I dedicate this book to my father,
Owen Otho Russell
whom I never knew. I love you, Dad, and know in my heart that we will meet again. If it had been God's plan for you to stay the course I know that I would have been proud of you.

I hope I would have made you proud too.

And to my wonderful fiancée, Suzetta, who is now a very large part of my life. Thank you, darling, for coming to know our Lord Jesus, and making our lives complete.

The Right Way

A Journey Into the Light

Robert O Russell

Published in paperback by Belief Books 2011
www.belief-books.com
using SilverWood Books Empowered Publishing®
www.silverwoodbooks.co.uk

Copyright © Robert O Russell 2011

The right of Robert O Russell to be identified as the author of this work
has been asserted by him in accordance with the Copyright,
Designs and Patents Act 1988.

All rights reserved. No part of this publication may be reproduced,
stored in a retrieval system, or transmitted in any form or by any means,
electronic, mechanical, photocopying, recording or otherwise,
without prior permission of the copyright holder.

ISBN 978-1-906236-67-0

British Library Cataloguing in Publication Data
A CIP catalogue record for this book is available from the British Library

Set in Sabon by SilverWood Books
Printed in England on paper from responsible sources

SilverWood

The Right Way

It is only by God's grace that this book has been written. Without my heavenly Father having His hand on my life from an early age, I would at this moment in time, be without words and wisdom.

TO GOD BE THE GLORY

Foreword

This book is based on the life of the author. All situations are true and void of fiction, the experiences recounted here have happened to me personally. You will be taken on a journey of my life from about the age of eight. I have endeavoured to keep it as light hearted as possible, while still trying to get across the message that I hope to convey to you, the reader.

You may be someone who is an avid reader of anything. Someone, who is drawn by this foreword. Someone, who just liked the title, and has not given a thought as to what may or may not be inside this book.

Maybe you are just like I used to be where books are concerned and you buy what you think you'll enjoy when you retire. Yes, I was just like that. I never liked reading. I just bought them and stored them for later.

However, I came to a point in my life when I felt that God was telling me to put all down in writing, as He was not taking me on this life journey without a reason.

There is a Godly plan for us all and mine is not finished yet, so this book is not a complete life story. It will only be completed the day that I stop writing, which is not yet known.

I digress somewhat… sorry.

Whatever kind of reader you are, I pray that the Lord will touch your life in some way through this book.

At the very least, I hope it makes you think of one situation during your life, which you cannot understand, explain how it was accomplished, how you escaped or how you came through.

Believe me; we all have angels with us, as I will testify to in this book.

I do not hold with political correctness and therefore make no apologies for offence caused because an individual, organisation or other does not like the way a section has been written or a particular word used.

We live in a free country, at the moment anyway, although others seem to have different plans. Plans that do not in any way fit with the plans of our God in heaven.

Not everyone can read between the lines and actually see what is being said, but the Spirit of our Lord is within these words, and I pray all who read them will be truly blessed.

Aside from all the reasons above, this book I feel in my heart God wanted me to write, to help all of you out there in the world who have found yourselves in a similar position as I did at some point, but have been unable for whatever reason(s) to come to terms with whatever happened, to accept and move on or worst of all, cannot forgive yourself or others.

Some things are an addiction, which can be brought on by our own making or peer pressure and the like, and some things are actually bondage.

I have been addicted and in bondage and neither is an easy lifestyle to admit to, but they can both be overcome with the love, grace and guiding hand of our Lord Jesus.

In my view, I was more fortunate than most. I had to go through what came my way and was shown a life of what not to be caught up in, so that healing could come to others in God's time. There are, of course, some scars, be they physical or mental. But God has brought great healing into my life many times. I have at times been very scared, out of my depth and in despair, but God has always been there even though I was not always with him.

I have no illusions of instant healing for thousands or even hundreds – that is for God to decide and God only. I do know in my heart that this book will show you that there is a God, a loving God, and that He wants nothing but the best for you, in this life and the next.

No matter what you are going through or what shame you may feel, God can heal all, and He has, by the death of His own Son, our Lord Jesus Christ.

> *By whose stripes ye were healed*
> 1 Peter 2:23
> The Rainbow Study Bible (New International Version)

God knows our heart and the person we are destined to be. I believe that God saw in my heart a willingness to bare my soul and be an open book for others. He has allowed my life to go the way it has up to now for He knew I would survive all because of His Son's grace and love for me and my love for Him. He also knows that one of the desires of my heart is to be able to heal others.

I spoke to the Lord about healing but I was referring to healing by the laying on of hands. As usual, God already had a plan and yes, it was for healing, but now I am sure it is for healing in a different way.

I believe that God will allow others who are suffering to a lesser or greater degree than I had suffered, to see their own personal plight within this book and through the words that are written find healing for themselves.

This book has, however, been written as a short autobiography so that you, the reader will learn more about me personally, and see how God has used and protected me throughout my life. As an individual I am sure that I have been seen by some as too easy going, gullible at times and far too soft hearted for my own good. This I will admit is true, but only if you go through life without faith. With faith in God, He truly can use the weak to confound the wise and has done many times in my case, I am sure. For in my weakness he is strong.

I will list a few of these instances at the end of the book.

Thank you Jesus, for your undying love, guidance and protection in my life, you are the one and only true God.

All names have been changed to protect the identity of those still living, and the memories of those no longer with us. May their souls be at peace.

Robert

My Favourite Psalm

The LORD is my shepherd; I shall not want.
He maketh me to lie down in green pastures:
He leadeth me beside the still waters.
He restoreth my soul:
He leadeth me in the paths of righteousness for his name's sake.
Yea, though I walk through the valley of the shadow of death, I will fear no evil: for thou art with me; thy rod and thy staff they comfort me.
Thou preparest a table before me in the presence of mine enemies: thou anointest my head with oil; my cup runneth over.
Surely goodness and mercy shall follow me all the days of my life: and I will dwell in the house of the LORD forever.

Psalms 23

Acknowledgements

There are a few lovely people dear to my heart that I need to thank, for various reasons.

Jesus you are my all, my everything, my first love. Thank you for your hand of protection over my life during those tumultuous years. Thank you for being my Heavenly Father in the absence of my earthly dad. I acknowledge everything good in my life is from you.

Suzetta! Thank you darling for listening, advising and being there to wipe away the tears in the beginning and during my/our journey, and for correcting my spelling and grammatical errors on the odd occasion. I have said that I will always be there for you, but you have shown me that you truly are my earthly rock. Your help in the writing of this book is appreciated without end. I will always love you.

To my mother, who lovingly offered me a home after my marriage ended, and for enduring all the silent times while I was upstairs in the office writing this book. Your fastidiousness towards anything that is not of the Lord has always fascinated me, showing you to have great faith in God's word. I pray that my own faith will continue to grow and in time will shine for God as yours does.

To my daughter, thank you for reading the draft copy and giving your input where needed, and yes – I did see the cringes on your face. It is widely known that sons and daughters are embarrassed by their parents, especially girls by their dads'. However, I hope you are able to see the reasons for this book and accept it for what it is. If not, then please humour me as you have always done. I love you and, as always, you continue to make me proud. May the love that shines in you, shine from your new born son, my precious grandson.

Danielle, thank you for the odd raised eyebrow, stern look and wide open eyes, which told me in no uncertain terms that I was wrong in what I had written or the way that I had written something and needed to think again. Continue to walk in the grace of God, Danielle, for you have the world at your feet, love in your heart and the love of God upon you. Your mother loves you, I love you, but God loves you even more. That in itself can take you to high places.

To my first wife, I hope you are not angry at your inclusion in this book and for being made part of written history. I would also like to take this opportunity to say publicly, that you were, still are and I am certain you will remain the best and most loving and attentive mother that any daughter could ever wish for. Time moves on and things change but I will always be proud of you. May God bless you beyond your wildest dreams throughout your future life.

To my brother, thank you for being there in the early stages of my marriage break-up. I felt your love and know it has helped to strengthen our relationship. Now though I am proud to be able to say, welcome to the family of God, may you grow in strength daily and live for the plan God has for you.

To my new grandson, I just want to say, my love will

always be with you.

Amazing grace: in loving memory of my dear departed sister, Rosa, whose faith was reaffirmed on her death bed. I know you are at peace, my love. I will see you soon.

To my niece and my sister-in-law, I pray you will both avail yourselves to read this book, and allow love and healing to come into your lives. God bless you both.

To my Spiritual mother and sister in Christ and loyal friend, thank you for all the time you have allowed me to take out of your day on numerous occasions. You were there in many aspects of my life to steer me in the right direction. You had me in your thoughts and prayers for over twenty years without even knowing me. Now we both reap the fruits of your prayers. You are a superstar and you know who you are.

To my pastor, I can only say thank you for being so on fire for God, your delivery of God's word every week, has been awesome, lively, comical, inspiring, impacting, mind blowing and life changing. You are a true leader and superstar.

There is bound to be some names that I should have mentioned but have not, nothing personal, I still love you.

Last but not least, to all my spiritual brothers and sisters who have become involved in my day to day life, along with your husbands, wives and your children, and my friends who don't yet know the Lord. I love you all as though you were my own and I am there for you. God bless you all.

Robert

Poem

I seek Him here, I seek Him there,
I seek my Father everywhere,
He's in my heart;
He's in my soul,
Eternal life is my goal,
With grass so green and air so pure,
New life will have such an allure,
He's set aside a place for me,
In my heart it's plain to see,
I know on earth there will be some strife,
But I'm written in the Lambs book of life.
The path is there it has been trod,
Walk in the steps of Son to God,
Just walk the walk no need to run,
Twill be best thing you've ever done.

R.O.R

Contents

	Foreword	i
	Favourite Psalm	v
	Acknowledgements	vi
	Poem (1)	ix
	Contents	
1	Touched By God	21
2	Loving Life	28
3	Purgatory	40
4	Steadfast With A Twist	54
5	Change Of Direction	69
6	The Wrong Approach	83
7	Paralysis	89
8	Life As Normal	99
	Poem (2)	109
9	The Way Home	111
10	Love From God	120
11	The Right Way	125
12	My View Of The Right Way	127
	Poem (3)	133
	Examples	137
	A Personal Word For You	140
	Afterthoughts	143

1

Touched by God

Be thou touched by my hand oh little child
Lest the ways of the world be dark upon thy flesh

I was born at home and delivered by my maternal grandmother, as the midwife had said that I was not due for ages and went home for her lunch. My grandmother knew this not to be the case, as she had delivered at least six other babies from what I know and was well aware that I would soon arrive. When I came into the world apparently, I had the amniotic membrane over my head. The membrane covers the whole body but comes off during the birthing process. I have been told that if it is left on the head, it becomes known as the amniotic sack. My grandmother knew what it was and quickly took it off so that I could breathe. She put it to one side with the intention of selling it to sailors, as she knew that the sailors considered it extremely lucky and would pay a lot of money for it. Unfortunately the midwife did not know that sailors would pay a handsome price for the sack and discarded it in the rubbish, unbeknown to my grandmother, until it was too late.

I have heard other stories that amniotic sacks have a

spiritual significance but have been unable to collaborate this in research. Having said that, I have been blessed with the gift of visions and revelations, which I feel may be connected with the amniotic sack. After all, God did create me in my mother's womb.

The very early years are somewhat sketchy or even mushy; however I will endeavour to recall what I can.

I was born on 13 December 1950, during the reign of King George V1; five and a half years after the end of the Second World War.

Maybe I should not have written it like that, as I now suddenly feel a lot older. Oh well, c'est la vie.

In some aspects of life at that time, the war years were still very evident. Clothing was hardly fashionable, certain foods were still restricted and bomb damage was still evident. Fortunately, though, not in the community in which I lived.

I cannot remember the death of King George V1 or comments through the media, or the normal word of mouth comments around the neighbourhood, but I do recall standing at the bottom of our road in 1953, waving my little Union Jack on a stick to the Queen and Duke of Edinburgh as they passed by on their tour of the country.

I was born at home, just outside the town of Gravesend in Kent England, into a life that would take me through many situations and ultimately to a new life. When I was eighteen months old my dad bought a property about five miles out of town. It was actually the outskirts of the town which was known as the rural area. My dad, mother, elder brother Matthew, elder sister Rosa and I all lived together.

I have virtually no memory of my father who died in 1955, although I know he was standing behind me when I was waving the flag at the Queen, despite having no picture of him in my head. I know, however, that he would have been there as my dad was an ardent royalist and would not have missed it for anything. Dad showed a keen interest in rearing poultry and in his thinking, was way ahead of his time.

Apparently, it was his desire in the beginning of the fifties (which my mother still has written on paper) to bring the chicken all ready to cook to the customer. I think Mum said he had been told that it would never catch on. I recall one day looking out into the hallway of Mum and Dad's bungalow and seeing a long line of cardboard boxes, which were full of tiny baby chicks chirping away. This was probably the start of his dream. What a shame it never got the chance to come to fruition.

I also remember an old pigsty down the bottom of the garden in which my dad kept geese. Maybe the former owner of the property used to keep pigs, or Dad just thought it would be a fun idea to keep geese in a pigsty. I can imagine that his sense of humour would have been a cross between mine and my brother's – rather wacky at times, to say the least. I remember going in the sty once and being chased by the geese but other than that, nothing. Apart from the above there is no more in the archive of my brain concerning this particular time in my life. However, Mum says to me that Dad will never be dead all the while I am alive, as I look exactly like him and many of my mannerisms are like his.

It is strange not ever having known my father, and therefore somewhat of a puzzle as to why at different times in my life, when I have allowed myself the time to ponder on what he may have been like, that I should become tearful.

I never knew him, but I do. Sometimes I have thought that Dad would not be proud of me and other times I think he would have been very pleased. Through what I have been told by my mother and seen in different photographs, I have built up my own thoughts of what Dad would have been like. I have very much increased my own volume of thoughts, as to what he was like while I have been writing this book. I have the feeling that he would have been the kind of father that any young man would have been proud of as his son. I know my own brother has memories of his own about our father, but he has never spoken a word about them. This, I feel is a painful area for him and pray that he will be released from that pain through this book and that he will be able to share his memories with me.

Nobody has ever said that my dad was a Christian man or that he ever attended church, but I like to think that what happened to my mother after his death was confirmation that he is with God.

A few weeks after Dad passed away, Mum was apparently at her wits end as to what had happened to him. She called out to God one night and asked him if Dad was alright. That night, Mum said her bedroom shone like a really bright light. Mum knew in her heart that God was telling her that Dad was fine. For now, I hold onto the thought that Dad is with my sister Rosa and God, and one day Mum and Dad will again be reunited. When the time comes that the Lord calls both my brother and I home, we will once again be reunited as a family, but this time as brothers and sisters in Christ.

Dad passed away in 1955 and his demise would over the years change the life of the family forever.

It is amazing what legacy you can leave for your wife

and children even in death.

The community in which we lived had no church, and Sunday school was held in the local memorial hall. Mum would take me there every Sunday morning for Sunday school and I would listen intently. In the months after Dad's death she turned to the Lord for help, as she was in turmoil at the thought of what lay ahead, being a widow at such a young age with three young children and a home to run. I would surmise that such a task would not have been easy during the male dominated fifties, and her heart must have been full of trepidation at the thought.

In the same year of 1955, a vicar moved to the area. Mum became friendly with the vicar and his wife and in these early days after Dad's death, she came to know the Lord personally. She became born again.

The vicar Mr Bright held Sunday services in the front room of the vicarage for the first few months that he and his wife were there, as they were unable to obtain permission to hold services in the local memorial hall.

Eventually though, permission was granted and services were held there, which was far better as more people could come along and hear the word of God.

I found out recently while talking to my mother, that Mr Bright never forgot Matthew or me, as he had stated in a letter that he had written to her, that we had left our mark on the back of his dining room chairs, and whenever he looked at the chairs even twenty years later he remembered the good times that were had.

Although permission had been granted to use the hall, the allowance of storage space was refused, so everything for the Sunday service had to be stored elsewhere. This problem was solved temporarily by the intervention of my mother.

Our bungalow was only one hundred yards along the road, so she offered to store the cross, alter cloth, communion chalice, hymn books etc at home during the week, and on a Sunday it would all be loaded into a wheelbarrow and taken down the road to the hall. I always wanted to push the barrow as it made me feel special, needless to say as a youngster, I did not always get my own way. This lasted for a few months until permission was eventually given for the church to use a cupboard within the hall, which was by far a better idea.

The year was 1958 and it had been agreed that a group would have occasional prayer meetings at the bungalow. At one of these prayer meetings, my life was the second one within the family that was to change forever.

Strange that a five year-old should sit in on a prayer meeting you may think, but after talking with Mum as mentioned above, she said that for a few months after Dad died, I would keep running in and out of the house shouting 'Mum, Mum' to make sure that she was still there and had not disappeared like Dad had. Now I know that this is three years further down the line, but had I become tied to her apron strings, or had Dad's death just made me very insecure?

I recall that my mother was having a meeting one weekday evening with the vicar and other members of the church. The vicar Mr Bright was an elderly gentleman, (well at my young age anybody over the age of twenty was elderly, so I would probably have seen him as a dinosaur). A lovely man from what I can remember, very gentle in his manner, kind and, for want of a better word, 'daddified'. I recall sitting in the living room while he was talking. On reflection, I feel sure he was praying. I recall my eyes suddenly welling up with tears, prompting me to rush out through the kitchen into the bathroom and shut the door because I did not want people to see me crying. Just after I had gone into the bathroom, Mr Bright knocked on the door and asked if he could come in. I remember he was talking to me for quite a while, obviously trying to explain to me what had happened and what it meant. I cannot remember what he actually said to me but I do recall a warm feeling and a wonderful calm coming over me.

Here I am, born again at such a young age. What did it mean? All I can tell you is that I knew without a doubt that Jesus loved me and that he was with me in whatever I did. The words 'born again' did not really mean anything to me then. All I knew was that I felt totally different and special.

Today, I suppose it would probably be classed as odd or weird, just as it was seen by some back then. However I would much rather be odd or weird than not know where I am going. I did, and still do, feel special.

Now you may think that is a conceited thing to say, that I felt and still do feel special. Well I am not deliberately putting myself above anyone else. Have you ever felt that you were destined for something other than what was the now in your life? That is what I mean, though I did not know it at the time.

2

Loving Life

Thy heart be of good breeding,
Command thee though, the ways of thine own flesh

My young life was great. Life at that time was certainly blessed, being brought up in the beautiful countryside and having a garden one third of an acre, in which to do whatever we wanted. My brother Matthew being two and a half years older than I, did his own thing, but I had the building bug from a very young age and embarked on many projects, all very unstable to say the least at the best of times.

As I write these next few paragraphs, I realise that even the things I was doing at this age was a training ground for later life. Some of the experiences, if not most, were teaching me how not to do something. You will see what I mean, as we go along the journey.

My first venture was to build a camp down the bottom of the garden, but this was a camp with a difference.

A hole approximately ten feet long by six feet wide was dug in the ground to a depth of about four feet. Then timbers were laid across the top and on top of them were sheets of corrugated iron. This was in turn covered over with some of the earth that had been dug out of the hole, and tufts of grass that had been dug out were placed on top for camouflage. 'There, all done' would have been my thought at the time, but then I remembered that I could not get into the camp, because I was above ground and the camp was below ground. I decided that I had to build a tunnel into the camp, so I dug down about three feet and about three feet away from the camp. I then tunnelled through to the camp. Naturally, by doing this the tunnel would have been sloping down into the camp, as I had not thought about rain water running in. I was so chuffed with myself, I crawled into the camp and finished off the inside, cutting out little niches in which to put candles, as it was so dark. When I had finished, I got into the tunnel to crawl out (and if you read between the lines, you'll probably know what happens next). Wallop! The tunnel collapsed on my head because I had not shored it up! In the crimpled folds of my mind, I can remember involuntarily eating dirt, followed by a slight feeling of panic. Eventually I managed to get myself out of the pile of dirt.

You are right of course, I was only a youngster. How should I have known any different? There is no reason why I should have done, but the Lord was showing me something that I would come to understand many years later and that was making sure that you build on solid foundations, do things correctly. In this case shoring up the tunnel, as I was taking a chance by relying on the ground to support itself without help; it could come crashing down at any time and it did.

Building on solid foundations is not just something meant for buildings or roads; it applies to anything in life.

Marriage, friendship, business, hobbies, faith, anything we build needs a solid foundation. If the foundations are solid then, whatever you have built has a far stronger and better chance of survival. If however the foundations are weak then it could come crashing down at anytime.

In 1959/60, the community was fortunate and privileged to have a Calvary crusade come to our area. They were there for seven to ten days, in a large marquee on land that belonged to a local family just down the road. I was totally enthralled by the speaker and can remember taking myself to every meeting that I could possibly get to. I tell you, the message that was given at those meetings when I was just ten years old still holds true for me today. Jesus died for my sins, so that I may have everlasting life. Yes, Jesus is alive today and living in my heart.

Around this time, sadly, Mr Bright moved away and a new vicar, Mr Sloan, came to the area. Eventually a church was built in our community and I became a member of the choir. I enjoyed singing as it always made me feel good. Digressing for a moment, don't worry you'll get use to it. Maybe that is why I feel that I want to start singing again. Having given up smoking after forty-eight years, it is something I keep thinking about and God does give us the desires of our hearts as you will also find out later. I used to sing with a police male voice choir and there is a CD out there with my name on it, along with many other names. We would travel to various areas at home and abroad to prearranged concerts raising money for different charities, and I enjoyed it immensely.

Home life was busy from time to time. Having no father and my mother having a full time job plus running a family home, I would often be seen doing jobs not really meant for a ten year old boy. However, they had to be done and one could not expect everything to be left to mother, so you just got on with it. Firstly, I painted the outside of the bungalow with the old fashioned snowcem that was in powder form and had to be mixed with water, then I helped Mum's neighbour lay a large concrete patio at the back of our bungalow. The preparation for the base took ages, but I was being shown how to lay a foundation correctly.

I started to do small jobs for other people around the area, which earned me a little money. One job I did on a weekly basis was to tend the garden of an elderly couple along the road from Mum's house. It was a big garden and there were many flower beds that needed tending and the lawns had to be cut and the edges trimmed in a specific way. Perfection was the word; the elderly gentleman liked his borders done a specific way and he would not settle for anything less.

Now you're probably thinking, what has this got to do with the Lord? Well I was being taught the basics of what would be good grounding for later life. I was being taught that if you take on a commitment you honour it, and the only way to build a base was with a good foundation. God was also showing me that there was a right way and a wrong way and we should never settle for second best.

It was around late summer 1961 and there was an old part of an orchard attached to someone's garden in another road. In this garden there was a damson tree and the damsons were ripe for picking. My mate Scott and I decided one Sunday that we would go scrumping for damsons (thoroughly recommended if you've never done it) so off we went down the road to the garden, over the fence making sure that the builders across the road did not see us go in. Good job they were there though.

The lowest branch was slightly out of our reach, so we looked around and found an old tin bath, which we turned upside down and used as a hop-up. Once up the tree, we started to pick those lovely damsons. Which reminds me, I haven't had any for years.

Anyway, we filled our pockets to bursting point and then we pulled out the bottom of our jumpers and filled them also. Too many damsons were enough and we started on our way down the tree. Scott went first, followed by me and just before he got to the ground he shouted to me, 'watch that rotten branch!' Too late, I already had one foot on it with my weight as well! Snap, crackle and pop so to speak! I fell through the rest of the tree and unfortunately for me, the bath we had used to help us get up was still there at the bottom of the tree turned upside down! Only thing was, around the bottom was a sharp metal rim on which it would normally stand, but this particular Sunday the metal rim was to become a temporary part of my head!

There I was, squashed damsons everywhere and blood literally gushing from my head. I can remember my hand instinctively going to the back of my head, as you do when you bang it. I took my hand away to look at it to see if my head was bleeding. My hand and arm were covered in blood! Decisive action was called for. My mate Scott and I quickly made the decision that we had better go across the road to the building site, as we both knew that an ambulance was needed. The workmen did a double take when they saw me. I can still remember to this day that the site stopped work, and men were rushing from everywhere to help. It was a hot day and they laid me down and put corrugated iron sheets around me to keep me in the shade.

In those days nobody thought about the corrugated iron sheets actually getting hotter, therefore making me hotter and my blood thinner. They were doing what they knew best and I thank them for that. They were kind men. Someone on the site had phoned for an ambulance, and my mate Scott had run home to let my mum know what had happened.

Mum came rushing down to the site, just as I had been put into the ambulance. I was pleased to see her and hear her comforting words. 'Oh trust you, I've just put the dinner on!' With those words ringing lovingly in my ears, and the eyes of all the workmen peering into the ambulance, the doors shut and off we went to the hospital. As I lay on the stretcher in the ambulance, I remember that all I could think about was if they would ring the bell. Alas, my childhood wish was not fulfilled – they obviously did not feel that my injury was serious enough.

Now I can see this differently, I realise how silly I was to climb up the tree in the first place. Or, I could thank God for sending an angel to break my fall so that I only cut my head open. Or, the workmen could have totally ignored me and thought to themselves, serves him right, nothing to do with us. But God had made sure that the workmen at that site on a Sunday had kind hearts for God knew what was going to happen anyway and yes, I do believe my fall was broken by an angel.

This was the first time that I had been to the hospital and the first time that I had been stitched up. I had seven stitches and I was proud of it! In some strange, childish way it made up for the bell not having been rung in the ambulance.

The second incident was only about two weeks after the

stitches had been taken out from the first injury. Mum had a friend that had moved away but was coming to the area for a visit. Mum asked me to go down to another friend's house to let her know about the arrangements. It had been snowing heavily as time headed through the autumnal months towards Christmas, and the un-adopted road had been replaced with a horrible new road and pavement. Our characteristic unmade roads and grass verges and dykes were never to be seen again because the area had been earmarked for future development. After a very long period of infrastructure, works of main drainage being laid and the new road network having been completed, nature's scars began to heal and the area gradually got back to normal life although it was never quite the same. The only attraction that I could see about the new pavement and roads was the fact that it was much better for making slides in the snow. A few of us local kids had been doing just that after school during the week that Mum asked me to run this errand for her. I said that I would go, and told Mum that I would take my bike, because it would be quicker.

The slide we had been working on was at the top of a hill, which made it all the more fun. As I approached the top of the road, I decided that I would ride down the slide on my bike. It was fun at first but the inevitable happened and the bike went out from beneath my legs. I started to slide down the pavement on my stomach, head first gathering speed as I went, and the bike following behind me. The first section of the slide was wide. The property that it went past lay back a little from the road. The second property though, was closer and the front wall around it jutted out further towards the road, rather like a dog's leg. Well, I hit this section of the wall full force with my head and knocked myself out! I remember lying on the ice for a while and recall seeing stars for quite some time, but eventually I came to and got to my feet after disentangling myself from the bike. Strange how there is never anyone around when you need them. I carried on down the road to complete my mission and the woman that I had given the message to gave a return message for my mother.

I headed for home, walking with my bike, as I did not feel too well. Arriving at home, mum asked me if I had delivered the message. I said 'yes' and was asked by Mum whether there was a return message. For the life of me I could not remember if there was or not. I reckon I must have been behaving a little strangely for a few hours, or it may have been a day, I'm not sure. I remember Mum making me stay in bed and the family doctor was called. After he had examined me, he gave the verdict that I had severe concussion and that I would have to stay in bed for a week. It actually turned out to be two weeks but I know a few days of that were faked by me, as I was enjoying the time off school.

The third incident really should have been captured on film. I can see it in my mind's eye as I write, and it looks like some kind of sketch that could have been from a Laurel and Hardy film. I had made myself a soapbox. Don't even try to fathom out why the word soap came into it. I have no idea even to this day, as there was no soap involved in the making of it. Some used to call it a go cart or push cart, but seeing as I am a non-conformist I'll stick with soapbox. For those of you who have no idea what I am talking about, I'll describe it for you.

My soapbox was a plank of wood about 1.6 metres long, 200 mm wide and 30 mm thick. At the back was another piece of wood about 800 mm long, the same width and thickness as the main body. This was equally spaced and rigidly secured through the centre. At the front, approximately 200 mm back, was the steering arm. This was another piece of wood, 800mm long and the same in thickness and width. It was equally centred but bolted through the middle so that it would move from side to side when pushed either way.

Once this masterpiece was created, the complete assembly was turned over and the wheels attached. The wheels came from a baby's push-chair, as did the axles it was attached to. Once the wheels were securely attached to their respective axles, the complete assembly would then be turned over onto its wheels. Through the top of the steering arm or movable axle, a hole was drilled on either side. Through the hole was passed a piece of rope, which was also securely attached and repeated on the other side. This was your steering wheel or steering rope. If you preferred, though, you could lie down and use your feet. If you were building a deluxe version, an open ended box would have been built just in line with the back wheels for you to sit in. If you were really fussy you could even put a cushion inside it for comfort. Mine, however, was the standard version with no frills.

I had been using my soapbox for a few days and was pleased with my creation. It gave me great pleasure. I decided on this particular day to take a ride along to the shops. As I approached, the husband of one of the shop owners was walking down the road towards a steep hill that went down and then up the other side. I went into the sweet shop, which was run by his wife. She asked me if I would go down the road on my little 'box thing.' Her husband had just left for work and he had left a letter behind, which he would need that day. I agreed to help, took the letter and off I went. I thought it would be quicker for me if I lay on the soapbox, my head towards the front, rather than the customary lying down position which meant steering with my feet.

I reached the top of the hill and gradually started to gain speed, which was proving to be a little more rapid than I expected. I remember that it seemed very fast. The fact that I was only about six inches off the ground made it seem even faster. I was out in the middle of the road, as there were a few parked cars down the hill. Now remember as you read this, we are in the year 1962 and the cars in those days were still made well.

As I approached the bottom of the hill, I had a feeling prompting me inside. I should have been controlling the soapbox with my feet and not my hands. It really would have been easier lying down with my feet at the front of the box – controlling the steering arm would be a lot more precise. It was, however, too late. I don't know if I hit something or just did not have a good grip. Either way, I lost control and the soapbox careered down the rest of the hill, rolling over a couple of times, and smashed into the rear wheel of one of the two parked cars at the bottom. I hit the car about the same time and just for a change I decided to hit it head first. The noise must have been loud because the shop keeper's husband who was near the top of the hill was the first person I saw. He stood over me and I remember saying that I had a letter for him. I offered him a crumpled envelope. I felt very sore for a few days but thank God, there were no bones broken. Even today I feel the urge to have a go. Unfortunately, health and safety plus legal implications may well impede my enjoyment – spoil sports.

The last incident, which was actually the first, I find very funny and if it puts a smile on your face then it was worth including in the book. I was nine years old and had never ridden a bike. My sister Rosa had outgrown hers and Mum said that I could have her fairy cycle, as it would have been known. It was a bigger bike than I should have had but I was sure that I could learn to ride it. The driveway down to Mum's bungalow was on quite a slope, not that long about twenty five feet and then a straight section of about ten feet. I decided one evening after school to have a go and try to teach myself to ride. I walked up to the top of the drive with the bike and turned it round to face the slope, then sat on it. I was just about to launch myself off down the hill, when I noticed a girl from down the road walking along the pavement. I know I was only nine and Tracy would have been about sixteen. She was a really pretty girl and for some reason, I just could not take my eyes off her. Now, when you have just launched yourself into some bodily movement, it can prove virtually impossible to stop yourself whilst in motion. Well, this was one of those times. I launched myself down the drive but what I forgot to do was take my eyes off Tracy, as she walked along the pavement. I just kept watching her as she walked past our bungalow and my eyes continued to follow her down the road. During this time the bike was still gaining speed down the slope and across the flat area. Still mesmerised by this vision of loveliness, my bike had lined itself up with its target because I was not steering. I hadn't thought about that. I suddenly turned to look forward just in time to see the bike's front wheel crash into the front wall of the bungalow, my face meeting the white painted render over the brickwork!

The bike looked sturdy enough when I got on it but after the collision, there was a pile of bike parts on the drive and me sitting next to them. My momentary vision of loveliness disappeared into oblivion. Another one for the comedy sketches, I concluded. I found out after writing this section of the book that my mum had seen the whole episode out of the window. She obviously thought it was a good laugh too, as she did not bang on the window to try and distract me away from my incorrect area of concentration.

I can imagine God actually having his head clasped in his hands and thinking, what are you doing son? Then having a heavenly chuckle to himself, as he probably often did with the antics of all his children. Even to this day, I am the same in some respects. I will leave my fiancée's flat and as I am walking across the road to the car park, I will turn my head and gaze up at the window just to see if she is looking. My guardian angels really are kept busy.

3

Purgatory

Life is full of traps and snares oh flesh of mine,
Be strong, Faith does conquer all.

Around this time, I was in the latter years of my junior school and I had seen over the years that certain boys managed to get jobs at lunchtime. They helped the caretaker take the school dinners from the kitchens over to the primary school and the girl's junior school and then to my school. Afterwards, they would go round and pick up all the empty plates and all the large pots that the dinners were transported in and take them back to the kitchen.

The caretaker, Mr White, was a grey haired old man (in the kindest sense), as he really was just short of retirement age. I was looking at the opportunity of helping him, as a way to get out of doing lessons everyday for an hour. Sadly though, the enemy (Satan) had other plans. I enquired about a job at the headmaster's office and was given a green light. Surprising, really, that I got it so quickly but as the headmaster lived just down the road from us, I think he may have had a bit of a soft spot for me.

I had not seen him, but there was another caretaker

who had only been there about six months. I was teamed up with him, as there was already a lad that helped Mr White. Now the caretaker who I was with does not really deserve a name but I will call him Mr Nasty, as that was what he turned out to be. Mr Nasty seemed nice at first, concerned for me and my safety. He would always reprimand me if I walked too close to the barrow in a certain position, in case I caught my heel on an area at the front which would have taken off all the skin on my heel (there was no such thing as health and safety then) and he would always ask me if I was okay whenever he saw me.

Looking back, I suppose he was being protective because he saw me as his possession. I remember the school putting on boxing matches as part of the sports week they had. The number of matches would be decided and then teachers would decide which boys would be matched together. There was never any guidance. You were just put in the ring with your opponent and a pair of boxing gloves, told to keep your head up and expected to fight. The matches in this particular year were on a Friday afternoon just prior to when I would go down to the boiler room.

When it was my turn, Mr Nasty had made it his business to be at the ring side, I suppose to be there for me between the rounds. Fortunately there were no rounds, as when the bell went the other lad came out all guns blazing, his fists lashing out in every direction nineteen to a dozen but my head was down and it was all I could do to keep myself from being pulverised! After the fight, of which I was naturally the loser, Mr Nasty could not wait for me to get to the boiler room, so he could touch me and make sure his possession was alright. I'm getting ahead of myself here.

When we had delivered the dinners, we would have

to wait about fifteen minutes and then pick up the dessert from the kitchen for delivery. These fifteen minutes would be spent in a little room attached at the rear of the kitchens. We would be on our own for about ten minutes and then Mr White would join us. There would be a roaring fire going in the cold weather, which was nice and cosy and in the winter months, I did not want to leave that warm room.

Mr Nasty used to give me sweets during this time and he would chat and try to get to know more about me. I thought he was really nice but little did I realise, I was being groomed, ready for his own personal perverted pleasure.

One Friday, after a few months, Mr Nasty gave me two shillings, which would be known today as ten pence. Naturally, I thought that was great, as I had my own money, as well as the sixpence that mum gave me for pocket money. This would have been two and a half pence today although the half pence was done away with years ago. This also carried on for a few months and all was well.

One day, however, during the break, Mr Nasty said he had something for me and beckoned for me to get off of my chair and go over to where he was sitting. Naturally, if that happened today I would not dream of doing such a thing, but having been brought up without my dad and Mr Nasty having been up to now somewhat of a father figure I thought I had better do as I was told.

As I approached him, he held out his arm, wrapped it around my waist and pulled me towards him. Nothing more really happened on that day except that when he heard Mr White coming, he let go and said not to tell anyone. I was scared, really scared and did not know what to do, so I did what he told me and said nothing. For a while, that is how it stayed. Every day he wanted to put his arm around me and then rewarded me just before the old man came in. I'm not sure how long that went on for, although I think it was only weeks not months. One day, as he had his right arm around my waist, he started to touch my bare leg with his left hand. I was wearing short trousers, which were worn as part of our school uniform at that time. Mr Nasty's hand slowly moved up my leg and under the hem of my short trousers. I was very scared, as I did not know what was going to happen next. To my relief, we heard Mr White approaching. Mr Nasty's searching hand was quickly taken away and he acted as if nothing had happened. The next day, the same thing happened. Mr Nasty beckoned me over to him and I obeyed. As usual, he put his arm around my waist and then started to run his hand up my bare leg.

On this occasion though, I am sure Mr Nasty knew Mr White was not coming into our room that day, as he seemed to have a slightly stronger grip around my waist, which I can remember feeling uneasy about. He allowed his hand to go even higher until it was on my underpants but not actually touching my genitals. I was scared but had learnt to put a brave face on every time he touched me. Now that he had managed to get his hand inside my trousers, he seemed content for a while and did not push any further. He did, however, give me a few extra pennies, which helped to take the pain away, so to speak.

After a few months, Mr Nasty asked me if I would like to help him on a Friday evening after school for an hour, locking up, picking up laundry etc. Obviously, being rather naive, I said yes. He offered to pay me two shillings and sixpence each week but this was the start of my real nightmare.

As sure as it was yesterday, I can remember thinking at

times, how I wished my daddy was here. Sadly though, he no longer was and being really scared, I just did not know what to do.

I started to go on a Friday night and Mr Nasty arranged to meet me after school at the boiler house, which was also the caretaker's workshop. I had decided that I should wear jeans for doing the work instead of short trousers as a way of trying to protect myself from Mr Nasty. So off I went to the toilets to change before going to the boiler house. When I got there Mr Nasty was waiting and we got stuck into doing the work straight away. It was not hard work, just rushing around to get it all done within the hour. When the work was finished, we would return to the boiler house. One particular Friday after entering the boiler house, I heard the key turn in the lock and my heart started to race. Mr Nasty started talking but slowly moving in my direction and I think out of instinct, I began to back away. He said: 'There's no need to be afraid. I'm not going to hurt you.' With that, he came over to me, took my arm and pulled me close to him. To my horror, he tried to kiss me on the lips! I remember him making several attempts to do so but I would not relax, so he stopped. He must have then decided that it would not be advisable to pursue it further that night so he paid me and off I went to go and catch my bus home.

I never spoke about this to anyone, as I felt sure that there would be a way out of it somehow.

There was a time when I was working in the boiler house, folding up the towels when Mr White came in. Mr White was a gentleman with white grey hair and he had one of those faces that was all screwed up, probably because he wasn't wearing his dentures. Anyway, he came into the boiler house to do something and he asked me whether everything was alright, to which I replied rather sheepishly that it was.

Now, why did I not take the opportunity to get out of the situation I was in? Maybe it was because I had been told to keep it a secret in order to get treats and money. It boils down to this in my mind: I knew that something was not right but I was too young to understand exactly what it was. On the other hand, I felt I was being treated 'kindly' and I did not want to seem ungrateful. I was very confused because my feelings of gratitude were mixed with a lot of fear that comes from the enemy and not from God.

I went about my weekends and my school days but no one was any the wiser that something was wrong. Little did I know that in Mr Nasty's sick mind, he was already plotting something for the following week, as I found out Mr White was away on holiday and he would use this as an opportunity to make progress towards his ultimate goal.

The following Monday, I turned up for the usual dinner time routine but after the dinners were delivered and we were in the fifteen minute waiting period for the desserts, I noticed that we did not go to the room where we normally would. Instead, Mr Nasty said ,'Come with me, as I've got to feed my dog.' We walked across the girls' playground and through a metal gate, which led up a short winding path to the caretaker's house. We went round the back and through the back door, where I saw the dog. He was fed by his owner Mr Nasty, who then walked into another room with me following behind.

I can smell it as I type these words. The room had a real man smell to it, not dirty but a musty, sweaty sock kind of smell.

Mr Nasty sat down in what I presume was his favourite arm chair, situated approximately forty-five degrees to the window, which just happened to look out onto the girls' playground. He pulled me firmly towards him, then onto his lap. It was not until he pulled me onto his lap that I realised it was a rocking chair. He leaned back in the rocking chair, so it would be difficult for me to get off easily. He pulled me further towards him and pushed his lips against mine. I remember his face being all bristly and revolting. If I was scared before, I was even more so now! He kissed me two or three times and then pulled me back so that my head was on his shoulder and he was cuddling me. He seemed content with that and shortly after, we had to leave to collect the desserts and deliver them. Knowing now that this man was a paedophile, I wonder if he ever had any remorse over how he treated his young innocent child victims, as that is exactly what I was. A victim and I'm sure I was not the only one. Given the fact that he was employed in a school environment, he had the perfect opportunity to prey off young innocent boys or girls, although at this particular moment in time, boys seemed to be his preference.

How have I managed to cope with my memories about all that had happened? The answer is, bury them and bury them deep, so you cannot be hurt. As this kind of living nightmare progresses, you come to believe that it is your fault for allowing it to happen. You feel shame and fear at the idea of being thought of as weird if you're ever found out. Moreover, there is always the possibility that the one time your perpetrator actually does something or touches you somewhere that causes you pleasure, this helps to cement that you actually enjoy what is happening and want to be touched. These natural bodily feelings help the paedophile keep you snared within his web of lies, deceit, and perverted lust.

There is more to say about the hurt I experienced, but that will come later. Having been led by my Father in Heaven to write this book, I can say in all honesty that this has been a life changing experience for me. The reason I say this is because I have always had difficulty remembering minute details of past events from years gone by but somehow, having been inspired by God to tell my story, I have been able to remember detail and bring closure to a part of my life which has been buried due to my inability to cope with the shame and the fact that I blamed myself all these years for allowing it to happen. Naturally God has opened up the closed areas of my mind and given all the hurt back to me, along with all the tears, so that He can totally heal me. I am sure that during this recent return to the past, I was not the only one who shed some tears. I am sure that God has shed some too, knowing what the enemy has done to one of his children, and continues to do to others today.

Buried deeply for over forty-eight years, these memories are being brought back to me from the deep recesses of my mind, and are painful to recall. It is, however, total bodily and spiritual cleansing, for I can feel a difference in how I view the situation. There is still more to write, which may also be painful, but I have no doubt that total healing is being given to me by God through this book, which I know in my heart will help others when it is read.

The following Monday, Mr Nasty changed things somewhat. By this I mean he took things up a gear. After we had finished the first round of the dinner deliveries and gone to the room, he sat down and pulled me towards him but not onto his lap. He pulled me round to his left hand side, as I usually stood on the right and he put his right hand on my leg and started to work his way up. He then pulled me down slightly towards him and kissed me on the lips. As he did so, he pushed his hand under my underpants and started to fondle my genitals. This became the routine over the next few weeks and my genitalia had become his new lunchtime toy. On the Friday of this particular week, after the work was done, he could not wait to get his lips onto mine. He kissed me with a passion which should only ever be experienced with a girlfriend or a wife. For some reason he did not touch my genitals, as he had during the lunch break. Instead he said to me, 'Where do you change into your jeans, Robert?' I told him that I changed in the toilets before I came over. 'Well', was his reply. 'Next week, why don't you bring your jeans with you and get changed here.' I nodded sheepishly and agreed.

I found fear to be a strange emotion when it surfaced within the situation I was embroiled in. You're gripped inside by a strong desire to get out of a given situation which you're not sure about, but there is also a tendency to please, maybe because one is afraid of possible repercussions.

Mondays came round all too quickly for my liking and the week's routine started all over once more; nothing different – the same procedure every lunch time.

Friday came and I was feeling particularly scared, as I had agreed to go and get changed down in the boiler house. Okay, I hear you say, why do you have to get changed before going? I guess it's the fear of not knowing what might happen if I did not follow his suggestion, especially after I had agreed to.

I got down to the boiler house but he was not there. There was a written note on top of a big pile of school towels lying on the floor, which had to be folded and put into a large wicker basket. I did as instructed on the note and folded all the towels and placed them neatly in the basket. I don't know why it happened this way but for some strange reason, I did my work while I was still in my short trousers. By the time I had finished he had still not turned up and I decided to put my jeans on while he was not there, as it would be safer. I undid my trousers, let them slide to the floor and stepped out of them. Then I reached for my jeans to put them on. I put my right leg into them and as I put my left leg in, just like a praying mantis waiting to make the fatal leap on her victim, he came through the door and was across the room like a flash of lightning, his left arm around my right shoulder and his right arm under my legs. He lifted me up and swung me round to face him and sat me on the work bench. There I was sitting on the bench, my jeans hanging around my ankles, shaking with fear and nowhere to go. He leaned forward and kissed me and his hand went under my pants to my genitals. He kissed me harder and then parted my legs and stood between them. As he stood there his hand again went under my pants and he played with my genitals while also trying to lean forward to kiss me, but for some reason I would not play ball and kept shirking back so he could not kiss me properly. I remember the look of resignation in his face as he lifted me down to the floor. I did no more but pulled up my jeans and was ready to go home. I was waiting for him to give me my money but he had not finished yet. He came over to me and gave me a cuddle. While he was cuddling me, he shuffled across the floor with me in his arms towards the door where he turned off the light and shuffled back to the centre of the room. I could feel him fidgeting but I had no idea what he was up to because it was pitch black.

Suddenly, to his probable great delight and my utmost horror, he took my hand and placed it on his semi erect penis. 'Yuk!' was my first reaction, followed by 'what do I do?' Just as if he could read my mind, he whispered in my ear and said, 'just touch it gently'. I tried to oblige but it made me feel sick to my stomach. I remember it was very soft but also very thick and it scared me. He must have sensed that I was very uncomfortable and said, "You're obviously not ready yet."

My memory of this terrible episode in my life abruptly came to an end right there. I don't remember leaving that evening but I do remember meeting my sister's boyfriend on the bus home and he said, "How come you're wearing jeans to school, Robert?" Well, there is no way I was going to tell him what had happened, so I must have made up some sort of feeble excuse. As for Mr Nasty, I never went back. I dodged him, which was easy for a couple of months when it would be the summer holidays and time to move on. I was free at last, or was I? A few months later I left the school to go to senior school and was pleased to see that the caretaker was an old chap who was nice to everyone, from what I could see. It was good to have a new beginning in a new school without familiar unwanted faces from the past.

Two years had now elapsed and the school was told in assembly one morning that our caretaker had been taken ill and that a stand-in would be attending at certain times of the day. This news did not bother a school full of children from the ages of eleven up to seventeen, apart from one thirteen year old boy and that was me. I was concerned that it might just be a face from the past. Two days later I saw a familiar figure coming out of the boiler house. It was Mr Nasty and all the old memories came flooding back to me. I managed to stay out of his sight for that day and to my surprise and great relief I never saw him again.

It did puzzle me for a long time why, if I never went back after that particular day, I had not done so before? Not having an answer to this question only managed to help cement the thought within me that all this was my fault.

The legacy of that unfortunate encounter may have been short lived for some, or a lifetime for many. For me, it was forty-eight years. Things which happened later in my life could be attributed to the experience with Mr Nasty. Other incidences, like intimidation and more abuse, which followed later, left their mark as well. I wondered for a while whether the experience with Mr Nasty had in some way left me with some sort of look in my eyes or face that attracted men with a tendency towards their own kind. The full extent of the effect that it had on my life may never be known to me. I have used the past tense because there have been many floods of tears during the writing of this book, which had to happen so that I could be so open and honest.

Tears are a great healer and with the love and grace of God and the comforting arms and understanding of someone who loves you more than words can say, it brings about great healing, self forgiveness, understanding and acceptance. You are also then able to forgive your perpetrator, which is probably the most important thing of all. For you cannot receive healing if you are unable to forgive others.

When I was in senior school and around thirteen years of age, I was in a particular lesson which I think was music. I sat next to a boy in class whom I had never sat next to before. In this account, I will call him Jack. I had spoken to Jack quite a few times and I also remember that he was fairly good at religious education in school, as I was. I got the impression that he had been brought up in a good Christian family and was a nice chap, if maybe a little effeminate. During this particular lesson, Jack touched my leg with his hand and I can tell you, I was absolutely shocked. I remember everything about the Mr Nasty incident flashing before my eyes in quick motion, and right at that moment I thought that I was becoming the sort of person Mr Nasty was. I did nothing.

Sitting on one side of the classroom, our desk would have been visible to other pupils in the back row and I was aware of this but did nothing at the time. Jack began to move his hand across my leg and onto my penis and started caressing it through my trousers. Straight away I picked up the side of my jacket, which I still had on, and I tucked the end of it under the flap of the desk to try and hide what was happening. I did not really want him to touch me, but for some reason I did not take his hand away. I did my hardest to concentrate on the lesson and ignore what he was doing. It was only when I actually felt myself getting excited towards the point of ejaculation that I looked down, and to my total surprise he had managed to unzip my trousers and actually had his hand inside them without me feeling a thing. At this point, I pulled his hand away and all stopped, nothing was said and nothing ever happened again.

Around this time, at the age of thirteen, I got a job working on a local farm picking apples, mucking out the cow sheds and whatever came my way. One particular day, I arrived at the farm but there was no one around. It was pouring with rain but I decided to wait anyway. After a few minutes I heard a car coming down the track towards the barns and it turned into the courtyard. A man sat in the car and did not move for quite a few minutes but all of a sudden got out of the car and said, "don't just stand out there, Robert. Get in the car – you'll get soaked."

I wondered who it was but could not tell, as he had got back into the car. I went over towards the car and opened the door. He looked slightly familiar, but who he was I could not be certain. I really was getting soaking wet, so I jumped into the car. I was thankful to be out of the rain and just sat there looking out of the windscreen through which I could see nothing due to the very heavy rain cascading down the windscreen. I asked him who he was and he said, 'I'm Tim, you know me.' With that he put his left hand on my knee. Now it could have been totally innocent, just a friendly gesture, but I was taking no chances. I took his hand off my knee and said, 'I'll stand outside in the rain, thank you.' I got out of the car and walked towards the barn. The car started up and he reversed out and drove away.

All these incidents helped to bring about the bondage that I mentioned earlier and I'll go into that much deeper later.

4

Steadfast, with a Twist

Hell is where the flesh is, oh God raise me up.
The burning desire within me, doth search for life anew.

Being so young and having the faith that I had, intimidation was something that often came against me, and was one of many ways that Satan would try and destroy my faith. Young, mid years or older makes no difference to the enemy. He will try to kill, steal and destroy any way he can.

Sometimes intimidation is so subtle it's hardly worth a mention. It can be as small as just being excluded in some way, nothing actually said, but you know it is because you're different. You can feel like an outcast, or it can come in the form of old fashioned bullying.

Do you remember the old type of metal railing with the spikes on top, that was quite common in the fifties and sixties left over from the Victorian era? Well, one day at primary school, another boy who lived in the next road from me grabbed hold of me in the playground and bent my arms around the spikes so that I could not get away. He kept pounding his fists into my stomach, just because I was different.

A few years later the same boy at secondary school saw me with a badge on the lapel of my school jacket; it said THE LORD IS MY SHEPHERD. He cornered me on the stairs so that I could not pass and as I got close to where he was standing, he gave an almighty spit over the badge, and then walked away.

'So what, big deal!' I hear some of you say, and I agree – so what? It is not as if he had beaten me up or anything, but persecution – that was the name of the game he was playing. Small fry stuff you may say, but nevertheless, persecution.

There was a lesson to be learned from all the small and the bigger things that happened to me in my younger years. Some of us learn quickly in certain areas and some of us learn slowly. Unfortunately for me it was slowly, or perhaps this was fortunate. Maybe it was meant to be this way so that I grasped God's teaching and ultimately was brought to the point where I am today, writing this book in the knowledge that the Lord will use it to help others.

I have come out the other side every time and now that God is getting me to put it all down on paper, I can actually feel healing taking place within me, where it has not yet been done. You may be thinking why hasn't God, or if you don't know him, you might think, why hasn't your God totally healed you?

I cannot say why God does things the way he does, and it is not for me to question it, but I can try and reason it out – that is different. I know for my own part that in a few areas of my life I have had to admit to myself that it did happen to me, but no, it was not my fault, and I have also had to forgive any other person that was involved. Then and only then is God able to totally heal you. It is possible to get partial healing, which I had for many years but now that I know the reason why I only had partial healing, I want the full monty every time.

During the earlier years, when I was six years old, my mother had enrolled me in the Life Boys, which was the forerunner to the Boys Brigade. I used to go once a week and when I reached the age of about ten, I was promoted into the Boys Brigade.

This was good Christian grounding and helped me to grow stronger in my faith. I was proud to be a Christian although there were times when it was different. The Boys Brigade was not just set up to give young lads something to do. It taught good Christian values, discipline, respect and self control. It also instilled where it might be lacking, personal hygiene, team work and much more. Self control was something that I learnt the hard way in the Boys Brigade.

Over the years, I was promoted to lance corporal and then corporal. I was put in command of a gymnastics team for the evening. One particular young lad was deliberately messing about and kept getting out of line. Nothing serious, but due to my own inability to control the situation, which pointed towards bad leadership skills, I lost my temper and pulled his legs out from under him. The young lad ended up falling face first to the floor and his bottom two front teeth went through his lip. I was in trouble again, which was obvious, and I was instructed later in the evening by a sergeant that the captain wanted to see me.

When I arrived to see the captain, I was told that they had been considering me for promotion to sergeant but as I had shown a total lack of self restraint during the evening, this would now not take place. The punishment did not end there. Because I was good at gymnastics, they were also looking into sending me to a gymnastics training college, to train me as a gymnastics instructor. This too was an opportunity lost. The second opportunity lost may have been or could have been a life changing experience, so losing your self-control is not a good thing.

Our captain was an ex army captain, and the way he ran the Brigade may have seemed a bit too heavy for young boys. However, I can look back now and feel very proud of the fact that he was our company captain. God had put someone of good standing in charge and he was, in my view, a good role model. He knew how to be strict, but with love and he knew when to praise you and when to guide you. He knew how to have fun and would always join in. He would not suffer fools gladly and if he had the occasion to shout at you, ear drums would rattle.

I am rattling on; let me give this good man a name, as he was a good man. I'll call him Mr Joshua as Joshua was also a born leader.

Mr Joshua loved music and being ex army, he had a real passion for military music. Therefore, it was no surprise that he was our teacher for the company band. My personal passion was for the bugle, and after much practice I became convinced that my mouth was just not the right shape for this particular instrument. Mr Joshua suggested that I might like to try the side drum. It must have been something he could see, as when I tried it you would have thought I was born with one. I won't say that I was a natural, but I certainly had a flair for it.

When I started in the band, there were three of us on side drums but over the six years that I was drumming, we increased to five and I worked my way up to head drummer. Something I was proud of as a young man was winning the drummer of the year award four years in a row. As a company we entered competitions and won a few too. I spoke earlier about the gymnastics. I believe that all these areas in which I excelled were gifts from God. The strange thing is, in gymnastics I was best on the wooden box when doing the flying angel – a skill I was now unable to pursue. All the lads and officers in the company were great and we had lots of fun. We used to go camping each year, which was brilliant and we would have opportunities to do the Duke of Edinburgh's award at whatever level we were entitled to do. Sadly, I tried three years in a row to do my bronze award but I had a weak right shoulder when it came to throwing the cricket ball. I was always about five yards short, or four point two metres to be precise. Consequently, I never managed to gain the award.

We were also occasionally given a map, compass and different co-ordinates, dropped off somewhere and told to make our own way to the pre-determined meeting points. There were, of course, officers at different checkpoints for safety reasons, but unless we approached them for guidance, we were left to our own devices. This was always welcomed by me, as I enjoyed the challenge of finding our way to a certain spot, even if at times there were butterflies in my stomach.

One year, before the health and safety regulations came along and spoilt things, we were taken on a coach trip to an army training ground. We were there for the entire weekend, sleeping in the old barracks and on the Saturday we played war games with the army using thunder flashes – such great fun. We had been split into teams with soldiers and brigade members in each team. The team I had been assigned to had been moving through the woodland area for about twenty minutes, without any signs of the opposing teams. We came to a partial clearing, which was part of an old quarry and stopped. The army corporal in my team signalled for us all to stop and look around before trying to cross the quarry. Naturally, we obeyed his command. This was just as well, as someone spotted one of our brigade members in an opposing team. After about five minutes it was decided that all was clear, but to keep looking as we crossed. I helped the corporal getting the younger ones to go, aged ten being the youngest. Then it was my turn. For some reason I hesitated and I don't know why, so I ran. The next thing I knew, something landed in the hood of my anorack. Thankfully, the corporal was only about six paces behind me. He accelerated and grabbed my arm as he caught up with me, pulling the thunder flash out of my hood and throwing it. It exploded before it hit the ground. He looked at me and said, 'you lucky boy'. I don't think luck had anything to do with it – I know who was looking out for me.

One of the main things to come out of this weekend was learning how to be a team player. I personally learnt how important it is to look out for all who are in your charge, or just with you.

My earlier Christian values, learnt during my time in the Boys Brigade, had stayed in my head. I had learnt well in many areas but there were still many areas in which I had a lot of learning to do. The Boys Brigade motto was sure and steadfast; this I have always seen as being sure in your faith and that the Lord is steadfast.

During my time in the Boys Brigade, we used to go to summer camps to Bembridge on the Isle of White. In those days, times were tough for lots of parents, including my mother. Mum had on a regular basis been giving me money to pay in as subs for our yearly camp. On one particular occasion, she had given me five pounds to pay in, and lovingly said to me, 'be careful don't lose it.' Well I didn't lose it, as such.

At this time in my life, I also belonged to a judo club, and quite often would call into the clubhouse for a drink (only orange juice or lemonade was allowed of course) on my way to the Boys Brigade meeting. This particular evening I felt grown up because I had a five pound note in my pocket. At the clubhouse, I bought myself a drink – orange in a pint jug and if I remember correctly a bag of plain crisps with the little blue bag of salt inside.

It dawned on me that I had paid for them out of the money that Mum had given to me for subs, so you can just imagine what was going through my head. 'That's it, I'm dead, Mum is going to kill me!' These were just some of my thoughts. What was I going to do? (Devil speaking) 'Never mind, Robert. Why don't you use me, I might be able to get you your Mum's money back.' Of course, why did I not think of that, a gambling machine (one armed bandit).

There it was over in the corner, winking and smiling at me and saying 'come on Robert! Try me.' It was not like the big flashy machines there are today to entice people. It was just the old fashioned slot machine, but it had the same effect. In the change, I had a couple of sixpenny pieces, and in they went but nothing came out. Oh no, I've got to get those back I thought; more change required. I put more money in and got a little back – what a carrot that was. Again, more money went in, but alas nothing came out. This carried on for about half an hour, until all the five pounds had gone except for one sixpenny piece.

All the time this had been going on, God had not come into my thoughts at all, but he had not forgotten about me.

I do, however, believe that God allowed this to carry on so that I learned a valuable lesson. Now you might well ask, why would someone who is supposed to be an all loving God allow you to do something that could possibly get you in a lot of trouble. God knows the heart, and he knows how our lives are going to turn out. Being a young boy growing up without a dad, I was easily led and just maybe God knew that I would have got caught up in gambling so he needed to steer me away from it and He therefore knew the lesson would have the desired effect.

I was in turmoil, what was I going to do?

Oh well, I thought, in for a penny in for a pound, so I put in the last sixpence and pulled the handle. WHOOPEE! I won the jackpot, and guess how much I won?

Five pounds – miracle.

Thank you, Lord, for that very valuable lesson. Needless to say, I have not gambled from that day to this. I had learnt that gambling was indeed a mug's game.

I was now fourteen and my faith in the Lord was getting stronger. I was attending a Pentecostal church but had decided to attend their sister church which had a much more charismatic preacher. My religion had been recorded on my birth certificate as Church of England but I needed something much more vibrant and alive. This church suited me perfectly at that particular time.

The teachings I was receiving from both the church and the meetings we had on Sunday mornings at the Boys Brigade were building my faith, so I decided to be baptised by water. The Boys Brigade company I was in was partnered with the Baptist church. I spoke to our minister and told him of my decision. He was delighted and I asked him if he would come along on the day and to my joy he agreed. His face showed great pleasure, and I know he was truly happy for me. During the time leading up to the baptism, I carried on attending Sunday services and evening meetings.

The pastor at my new church was a young man, probably late thirties, but he was on fire for the word of God and his enthusiasm was infectious! I could not get enough. I was hungry and needed more. The day for baptism arrived and I could hardly contain myself. My family were there to witness the occasion along with the brigade minister, his wife and many members of the brigade. I felt very special indeed. Although other people were getting baptised as well, I felt that this was my day. The baptism took place during the afternoon, and in the evening I went to fellowship and was invited to receive the baptism of the Holy Spirit. "What's that?", you say. Well when you are baptised in the Holy Spirit you have the ability to speak in a foreign tongue to the Lord. You have no idea what you are saying, in my experience that is. In fact, it can sound like a lot of gobbledegook, but God knows what you are saying.

Now receiving the Holy Spirit is being given a gift from God, and that gift was being able to speak in tongues. Along with the gift of tongues comes the fruits of the Spirit, consisting of: love, joy, peace, patience, kindness, goodness, faithfulness, gentleness and self-control. If only those things had been given to me earlier. All things in God's time.

I thought my faith was strong, but obviously it was not strong enough. It was also misplaced but I will mention that in a later chapter. This was the start of forty years in the wilderness for me, although I never once forgot my faith or denied Christ, but I did, however, drift away from the church in a big way.

At the age of seventeen, I learnt that you really have to be careful what comes out of your mouth. My mother had gone to great lengths to secure for me an apprenticeship with the national gas company. In our area they were known as Segas. It was not what I wanted to do, as I had always dreamt of being a blacksmith. It was something I was really interested in and truly enjoyed the work that I got to do in the workshops at school where we had our metal work classes.

The careers teacher at school advised Mum when we went for the careers evening that being a blacksmith would not be a good job for me to go into. It was a dying trade he said, and there were much better opportunities in the work sector for me. How wrong that teacher was.

The apprenticeship with the gas company was agreed and I started in September 1966. I stuck with this for two and a half years, after which I quit my apprenticeship for a girl. This saddened my mother greatly. My mother had gone to great lengths to secure an apprenticeship for me and now it was about to be thrown away by the whim of a teenager. Mum tried everything she could to dissuade me from leaving. She even got the head of the southern region to try and talk some sense into me, but alas, it all went in one ear and out of the other. I had turned my back on one of the better opportunities of my life, by saying 'NO' (typical teenager). This was all done because I was intent on getting married to the girl I was dating at the time, and we had decided that we needed to earn more money.

There was good money to be earned at the Ford plant in Dagenham, Essex, at this particular time, so the apprenticeship had to go. The fairer sex had won this battle and the apprenticeship went. I stayed at Fords for about six months and during this time, I also worked for my fiancés father on Saturdays to earn a little extra money. The work was quite heavy and although I was not a weak teenager, I was like a lot of young men and wanted to be the Charles Atlas of my home town, so everything I had to lift during the day on my Saturday job, I tried to lift even more.

On one occasion, I doubled up on what I was carrying, which would have amounted to about 168 pounds or 76 kilograms. Although I managed to lift it, damage was done and during the rest of that day, I noticed a slight pain in the base of my abdomen which gradually got worse. This was verified to me when later in the day I went to the toilet and noticed that I had three testicles. We went to find a doctor who would look at me on short notice and his conclusion was that I had split the base of my abdomen open and my intestines were dropping through into my scrotum, apparently known as a strangulated hernia. A truss had to be worn for a few months, until I was taken into hospital for an operation. In those days it was a two week stay in hospital and a long time off work. The doctor in fact kept me off work for eighteen weeks, and after this I had to leave Ford and find another job, which was not too heavy. Needless to say, the big money was not forth coming for enough time to make a difference.

I managed to find a job closer to home working in the laboratory of a paper mill, but not long after this, my engagement broke up and I had to pay back a loan that I had taken out to buy a new van, which put me back to being broke and in the position of not being able to pay my way. This was the start of a downward spiral.

Was I headed for big trouble or had the Lord sent an army of angels to look over me while I was in the wilderness? I think it was both: being protected and learning many valuable lessons.

During my teenage years, I got into many scrapes of one kind or another. It was accident after accident with different cars and losing money all the time while getting deeper into debt. Over the period of ten years I was in endless trouble with the police with appearances in court and demands from the bank. Poor Mum must have been in total despair. As mentioned above, during this period the accidents were endless, with many appearances in court for motoring offences, with drink driving at the top of the list.

At this particular time I was nineteen and the situation took place on a Saturday night after a good evening out. I knew I had been drinking but had no idea how much had passed my lips. I can remember everything that happened but I also know I was out of control and unstoppable. On leaving the venue, five of us piled into my car and off we shot to the home of one of my mates. I can remember being so relaxed without a care in the world, driving like a maniac on and off the pavement, in and out of street lamps. Nevertheless, we arrived safely and totally unscathed!

I remember someone once saying something about a baby-sitter who had to be picked up. I can recall jumping on top of someone's parked car, running across the roof, sliding down the windscreen and the bonnet, jumping into my own car and speeding off before any of my mates could catch me. I can tell you now that I had no idea where I was going, as I did not even know where the baby-sitter was!

Off I went down the road. Just around the corner was a hill and cars parked on my side of the road. I pulled over to miss the cars but unfortunately there was another car coming up the hill, the driver of which was obviously in the same state as I was because he was driving in the middle of the road too. I swerved to miss him but unfortunately hit a parked car with great force. This car was pushed down the road into another car which also went down the road into another car, so including my own, four cars had been damaged.

As you can imagine, I was now wide awake and roared off down the road turning my lights off as I went. My downfall was stopping at the end of the road to make sure there were no cars coming, which of course there weren't. One of the neighbours, a woman, had shot outside like lightning and ran down the road. Just as I was about to drive off she tapped on my window and said, "Oh no you don't!" Being the soft, kind hearted, obedient young lad that I was, I stopped.

The police were called and I remember that breath testing had only recently come into force. The officer sat me in his car and produced a little plastic bag with a mouth piece on the top. At the bottom of the mouth piece were some crystals through which your breath travelled, and the result of this roadside test was dependant on the colour of the crystals once you had blown into the bag. This determined whether you were arrested or not on the suspicion of drunken driving. I will never forget the deep voice of the officer who dealt with me. "My my," he said, "we have been drinking haven't we." The crystals had turned the darkest colour possible and I was promptly arrested. A blood test was then taken down at the police station and sent off for analysis. I was also given a sample for independent analysis if I so felt inclined. The blood test came back positive – more than twice the legal limit for that time!

Eventually, I went to court and the magistrate said, "On this occasion, son, I am going to make an example of you." I was the second person in the area to be charged with the offence and I expect she thought by making an example of me the public would be deterred from doing the same. I was fined one hundred pounds, plus eighteen pounds doctor's fees and banned from driving for one year, with an endorsement on my licence – I was gob smacked! This was in 1968: I was only eighteen and I thought to myself, this will take me a hundred years to pay off! None of this, however, made a difference to me at the time.

Why then, do teenagers think and act in this way? I cannot really comment for the girls, although it might be the same. Firstly, we think we are invincible and that nothing can hurt us. Then, if we have older friends we cave into a certain amount of peer pressure. The best reason is that we speak out with great confidence in what we are saying: 'I'll be ok, not a problem, I can do it', but inside we are in turmoil and cannot speak the truth for we fear it will make us look silly in front of our friends. As such we do not address what is really going on deep inside.

As the years go by, all these little things that have been buried deeply grow inside us and gnaw away at the goodness we possess. We become bitter and twisted, because we do not know how to put things right without looking silly. Naturally, we do not want to look silly so we put on a brave face. There is however, an answer.

I carried on in the same way, drifting from job to job, getting into debt and more trouble with the police. By the time I was twenty-one, which was only four years from when I got my driving licence, I had had five road accidents. Thankfully nobody suffered from bad injuries.

I can recall a near miss when I had the van I mentioned earlier. I was with a mate and we had been out for the day. On our way home we came down a road which is known as seven mile lane, although it is now split into two sections by a roundabout. Being young, seventeen and full of testosterone, I was showing off to my mate who had not as yet passed his driving test. Two thirds of the way down seven mile lane there was a sharp right hand bend. This bend is now protected by a crash barrier but on the other side of the hedge, which is all that was there in those days, was a sharp drop. I have not measured it, but from memory it must have been at least forty feet.

Anyway I am getting ahead of myself again. We hit this bend doing about seventy miles per hour. Thankfully, my reflexes were good although my driving skills were not. I hit the brakes, sending the van into a right handed spin which I managed to bring to a quick stop. With adrenalin running very high indeed, we both got out of the van to seek instant relief at the nearest hedge. God was definitely looking out for me that night.

5

Change of Direction

The passage of life does wend its way
and will end up where,
One cannot say.

I was working in the paper mill that was mentioned earlier, to get a break from the rollercoaster ride of destruction that I seemed to be on. At this time, I also had my first inspiration to write a poem, but more about that will have to be on the Lord's direction.

Someone came up with the idea that I should become a bus driver. I cannot remember who it was, other than that it was one of my work colleagues. Some chance, I thought – with my record they would probably have a good laugh. I applied to London Transport and after a while received a letter back from the Metropolitan Police at Scotland Yard, signed by the then commissioner. The letter said in no uncertain terms that all the while he was the commissioner, I would never be granted a psv licence and that I should never have been given a driving licence in the first place.

Well, you can't blame me for trying. I decided to apply to the Maidstone and District bus company in Kent and was given a break. I started as a bus conductor and after a few months was eligible to apply for the driver training. I was accepted and completed my training, passing my psv (as it was called then). I soon got bored with bus driving, so I decided to give coach driving a try. Great I thought, having heard stories about coach drivers and all the women they got. Well, this was certainly true in my case: married women, single women, soldier's wives... the list was long and not good.

My black hole was getting deeper and darker. In my heart I was in turmoil. What was Jesus thinking of me? I convinced myself that it would be ok; I was young and only having a bit of fun. I was now in my twenty-fourth year on God's earth, and had been from one coach firm to another, but was now working for a company in Biggin Hill, Kent, and settled for about three years. One day when I arrived at work, I found that I had been hired out to National Express for a day, along with another driver. I was always one for rocking the boat if I did not like what the company had done. I said my piece and let them know that I was not happy about doing the job. As usual the manager won and off we set for National Express in London.

We went up to Battersea in London which was our first pick up point. We were to take employees of the London Electricity company down to Brighton for the day and then onto Dorking for a disco. The weather was lousy all the way there, pouring hard with rain. On reaching Brighton sea front, we parked up on the side of the road. I got out and went to talk to the other driver. While I was standing out in the pouring rain talking, the other driver was comfortably sitting in his seat. I was drenched. Saturated! but all of a sudden, I noticed something, or should I say someone.

Suddenly my world was to take a turn in a direction that I never thought would happen to me. You could have knocked me down with a feather. I could not believe what was about to happen to me. There I was, standing in the rain, talking to the other driver when I had a feeling that someone was watching me.

A young girl on the other coach was looking at me through the coach window, laughing and pointing at me. She was talking to her friend in the seat next to her, probably saying something like, 'look at that silly old man' (well I was twenty-six after all). I did not see her all day, but when we went to the disco in the evening, she was sitting with her friend at a table right at the edge of the dance floor. I looked at her and instinctively knew that this was it; I was in love! I said to the other driver, "You see that girl over there; I'm going to marry her." I know he thought I was crazy, but I just knew.

I went over and asked her if she would like to dance and she said yes. Her name was Chrissie; we started going out even though there was a nine year difference between us. Chrissie was a few weeks off becoming seventeen and I was nearly twenty-six. We went out with each other for about a year even though some of her friends were convinced I was a married man. Her sister also thought that I was married or had been married, but fortunately Chrissie took no notice, and we were married one year later. Two and a half years later, our wonderful baby daughter Shelly was born.

During the period we were courting, my black hole actually got deeper for a while and I came to a point where I thought I would spend many years in prison. During this time I changed my job and was working for a firm near to where I lived. One particular day I was travelling along a major road through the town, when all of a sudden I saw someone heading towards the crown of the road. I started to break but was pretty sure that the person had seen me. To my horror, the person kept walking and my coach ran into them, knocking them to the ground. The trauma of actually knocking someone to the ground is bad enough, but it is worse still when you see the actual injury taking place before your very eyes. If that was not enough, I was also put in the same ambulance and had to endure the sound of this person fighting for their life while we were transported to the hospital. Sadly though, this person died a week later from the injuries caused, and an inquest was called for.

The time heading up to the inquest dragged but eventually it was upon me and I was relieved although scared. I just wanted this horrible period in my life to be over. Although coroner's court is not as formal as crown court it is still not a very pleasant experience – especially when the coroner gives a verdict of death by misadventure. I felt scared but did not know what for.

I spoke to my barrister and asked him exactly what the verdict meant. He then dropped a bomb shell that I did not expect. He said that the case would be handed back to the police and that they would have to send away evidence of my skid marks to determine my exact speed at the time of impact. What would happen if it was decided that I had been speeding at the time of the accident? He told me that the actual speed of my vehicle leading up to the accident was not of concern any longer. The police now had to determine my speed at the time of impact. What if I had been speeding on impact I enquired, and he told me that in that situation, I would be looking at a charge of manslaughter. So now I just had to wait for the police to get in touch one way or the other. It was three weeks from the time that the police sent off all the measurements and information that they had, until I heard anything more.

Believe me that that was, and always will remain, the longest three weeks of my entire life. Every day I woke up and had that horrible feeling you get in the pit of your stomach. I could not concentrate. I went to work, but every time I tried to drive a mini bus, never mind a coach, I could see people walking off the pavement. I did not go back to work the second day but of course, I still had all the feelings inside me. On the third day, one of the other drivers who was a really nice guy came round to my mother's and took me to work. He gave me a good talking to and made me get into a mini bus and drive it. I can remember we were out for a couple of hours and when we got back, he made me get straight into a coach and go out in that. Even though he is no longer with us, I would like to say that if it was not for him, I would never have got behind the wheel of a coach, mini bus or car ever again. The letter came from the police and I was petrified to open it. Eventually I did, and the relief on my face must have been very evident. The police analysis of my skid marks showed that the coach was doing 29.9 mph on impact. This meant that I was speeding prior to the accident, which I was not happy about, but nevertheless I was within the legal limit on impact and that was good news. Lastly at the bottom of the page was the customary phrase, 'no further action will be taken on this occasion'. That was music to my ears and all other body parts that had been in shock for weeks.

Yet again, God was with me in the situation, but I had learnt a valuable lesson. Speeding is dangerous! I am not whiter than white where speeding is concerned. Far from it, because I do like speed, what I will not do now is speed anywhere that is a built up area, or where there is the likelihood of pedestrians walking out into the road.

Now if that is not the power of God at work looking after me, I don't know what is. I hear readers saying, 'you were just very lucky'. Well, I give no credence to the word lucky, as it derives from the word Lucifer, which means Satan or Devil or the enemy, as many including myself prefer to refer to him, and the enemy is real. Trust me, I know.

I recall when I was about ten years-old one of the youngsters in the area in which I lived was called Donny or Don Don. Many years later when I was in my early twenties, I got friendly with a chap and I spent a lot of time with him and his family. One such evening someone suggested having a go on the Ouija board and we all agreed. To be honest, I had no idea what an Ouija board was but remember having an uneasy feeling in my stomach. The board was set up and a glass was put in the middle and we each put our forefinger on the glass. The first attempt was a farce, as one of the party must have been a total skeptic and was trying to put the frighteners on us by rattling the table underneath. Then we had another go and after a while the glass started to move.

"Ok", I said, "who's moving the glass?"

"Nobody", someone else said.

We all agreed to put our other hand on the edge of the table. Again the glass started to move. first of all it went to the letter 'D' then it went to the letter 'O' and then the letter 'N'. We all looked at each other but none of us showed any recognition towards the word. The glass started to move again and it went to the letter 'D' then to the letter 'O' and finally to the letter 'N'. It suddenly dawned on me what it had spelt out and I quickly took my hand away from the glass and left the table. I felt uneasy about the episode and a couple of the others felt a little shaky, but we all managed to put the experience behind us.

I have thought about it a few times over the years but could not substantiate it with anything that I had heard. About five years ago I bumped into a relative of the same family and we were discussing old times. He was around my age and we had on occasion played together. I casually asked him how Donny was and was told that Donny had died a while back. I had no need to pry any further as my fears had been proven correct, from when I first saw that name spelt out on the board.

For the first few years after Chrissie and I were married things were a bit tight, but we were happy. I had work and Chrissie had a part-time job. Although I was unequally yoked in my marriage as my wife was not a Christian, blessings were always in abundance. This was mentioned on more than one occasion by my wife, and later my daughter. They would say, 'how come nothing ever seems to go wrong for us?' and I would tell them the same each time: that we were covered under the blanket blessing – the covenant that God had made with Abraham – that the Lord had given to my mother for her family. I am extremely happy that my daughter, at the same age as myself, gave her life to the Lord when she was eight years of age, although she now says she does not remember.

A Billy Graham convention was being transmitted to the big screen at our local theatre. My mother asked Chrissie and Shelly if they would like to go and they said yes. The end of the convention brought the customary heart warming music, and people were asked if they would like to come forward and give their life to the Lord. Shelly apparently tugged her mum's arm and said she wanted to go up. I just wish I had been there at the time. Chrissie told my mother that Shelly wanted to go up, so Nan lovingly obliged. That evening my mother rang me to recount to me how my daughter had given her life to the Lord.

Praise the Lord, my daughter was now covered by Gods grace! Now though she is not a practicing Christian. She is young and has decided that she wants to do her own thing. That is fine, for God gave us free will and we are at liberty to choose free will if preferred. Praise God though, she is not denying the Lord, and once you give your life to the Lord he will reign you back in when the time is right. It is only if you totally reject Jesus as your Lord and savior, and refute that there is a living God that you would not be saved. In my opinion, God gave us all free will and allows us to follow our own path, but he will keep tugging at your heart strings, and when the time is right will pull you back in line. I do feel somewhat ashamed though, that I was not in a strong spiritual position personally to guide Shelly on her spiritual path, as this is part of a father's role. What a blessing it is, however, to know that your only daughter is saved by God's grace, and I know in my heart that she will come back to the Lord in his time.

Blessings and miracles come in all shapes and sizes and time periods. God's angels are everywhere and I am glad they were on this day. My wife and I had gone to Florida for a vacation, one week in Orlando and then onto St Petersburg for a week. While in St Petersburg we decided that we must catch a baseball game. We heard that there was a home game on, just outside of the town the following evening, so we decided that in the morning we would venture out and find the stadium, as we did not want to get lost in the dark trying to find it.

The morning came and off we went to find the baseball stadium. We had spoken to a couple of staff at the hotel before leaving, but you know how it is – you listen to the directions that are being given to you and afterwards you're not quite sure, so you ask someone else just to double check and you end up being more confused than before you asked the first person. I knew there was a left and a right so we drove down the entrance road to the hotel and then turned right. All the roads on the left looked like side roads, although about ten times wider than ours would be in England, so we kept going till we hit a main road. Sure enough, after a while we came to a large intersection at the first set of traffic lights. We decided to turn left. Eventually, we arrived at the stadium and it really wasn't that difficult. Once there, we decided that the evening journey would not be difficult and it could be done blindfolded. We had pulled into the stadium car park and sat there for a moment or two just going over the route back to the hotel in our heads. Suddenly, I realised we should turn right out of the hotel, travel for half a mile to the traffic lights at the main intersection, turn left, travel for three blocks to traffic lights and then turn right. The stadium was half a mile up the road on the left. "What could be easier?" I said to my wife, and she agreed, but we decided that we should retrace our steps back to the hotel just to be sure.

Off we went out of the stadium and turned right, before driving half a mile to the traffic lights and turning left. We then travelled for three blocks to traffic lights on the main intersection and turned right, down to the hotel entrance on the left. Very simple, I was confident that there would be no problem later. We enjoyed the rest of the day just lazing by the pool until it was time to set off later in the afternoon for the stadium. Once there we had a little look around, a bite to eat, and spoke to some of the local people. We had about forty-five minutes to go before the match was due to start, but were reluctant to go for a walk around outside the stadium as it was not a safe area if you were not a local. The game was great. We had a brilliant time, but the Lord had other things on his mind concerning the return journey. God knows the beginning from the end – well it was certainly true in this case. We left the stadium and started our journey back to the hotel. We went out of the grounds and turned right, drove half a mile to the traffic lights and turned left. (Am I right so far? Go on, have a quick look up the page to see if I am going in the right direction. Okay, right on we go). We carried on for three blocks, and had gone about one block when my wife said to me, "Oi, you're going the wrong way, we passed that building on the way down."

I said, "I know we did."

She said, "Yeah, but it should be on the other side, it was on this side when we came down earlier."

Well, you could have smacked me in the eye with a wet kipper – she was right AGAIN! Still, I kept going and eventually came to a set of traffic lights. Ah, I thought. Turn right, go down the road for half a mile and the hotel will be on the left. I was thinking that the building we saw was similar to one this end. Half a mile down the road what did we come to? Yup, you got it; the baseball stadium. What had gone wrong? We turned into the stadium and took a few minutes to think about the way we had gone out and it had been correct. Off we went again, out of the stadium we turned right and carried on for half a mile to the traffic lights. Here we turned left just as before and just after one block, we came across lots of flashing lights. I had never seen so many police cars in one place. We were signalled by a patrolman to proceed and we did so, carefully rubber necking as we went by.

On the sidewalk was a man spread eagled and beside him was a large gun. Now, you can draw your own conclusion but I know that the Lord had taken us out of the situation, as we may have been in the line of fire. We had been taken back through time for our own safety.

Here is another miracle. Some of you if not many of you, may be able to relate to this. You know when you are on the motorway and all three lanes of cars are travelling fast and there is no room to overtake or pull in? Well, I was in exactly that sort of situation on the M25. There I was, in the outside lane doing 70 mph. All lanes were solid and travelling at the same speed. Suddenly I saw brake lights come on about three cars in front and smoke coming from its tyres. I anticipated what would happen, so I hit the brakes. The brake lights in front of me came on, and I can remember thinking, well that's it, I don't stand a chance! Suddenly, the steering wheel was taken out of my control. I thought at first that something had gone wrong with the car, because I tried to move the steering wheel but it was solid. I was looking out of the windscreen all the time and saw absolutely nothing, but within seconds I was in the middle lane doing a much more respectable speed, and there were no cars around me to the front, back or sides for about twenty yards. The Lord, through his Angels, saved many people from harm or even death that afternoon and although I may be the only one who knows it, thank you Jesus!

Anyway, I am getting ahead of myself now. Let me take you back a few years just to show you how life can turn out for you, but what Jesus can do for you when the right moment approaches.

As previously mentioned, I was a coach driver and this relates to that time. Well, I decided to re-train, as I was getting married and needed a better job with a better income. The training continued into the first six months of my marriage. I eventually qualified as a plater/fabricator and structural steel engineer. This enabled me to get a fairly good job in a fabrication factory. Lots of overtime was available and we were able to buy our first house after six months of marriage, although we had to borrow money for the deposit. After four years of being fortunate enough to be doing something that I really enjoyed, because I was actually using my hands and being creative, engineering took a dive in this country. The company I was with was being sold to another company, but there was not a position for me. I decided to get out before the sale. I applied for jobs in the same field and even walked into factories to ask directly if there were any vacancies. The answer was always the same: sorry mate. Well, it was good while it lasted but nothing lasts forever, not within this world anyway. I had to get my thinking cap on fast, as I was now supporting my wife Chrissie, and newborn baby daughter Shelly, and of course paying off a mortgage.

I thought long and hard about what I was going to do and eventually came to the following conclusion. Having always been good with my hands, I decided to start up on my own in the construction industry, doing building work and maintenance.

The first few years were touch and go. It's often the case that when you are still fairly young and green, things like red reminders, no money, bailiffs at the door and the threat of house repossession become familiar concepts. We had some rough times but they did not last long and helped to make me stronger.

The next three years were much better. We were able to start putting our finances into better shape and move to a better house in a better area. Life was good again and everything was running like clockwork. Then the country was hit by recession and I was forced to think about giving up being self employed. I did not want to do that as I was enjoying the freedom of being my own boss, even though it did have its down sides.

Fortunately, my daughter was at a private school and the father of one of her school friends was an accountant for a development company. We had become friendly through the children going to each other's homes for sleep overs and all the other things that children do. We were invited to dinner one evening and I was asked if I would be interested in working for a construction company. I was invited to go and meet a manager on site to have an informal interview. We got on well and I was offered a contract to do all the maintenance on new properties that were covered under the National House Building Council's two year Building Maintenance guarantee. I carried on doing the contract work for about a year, during which time the company had increased their volume of work considerably and I was offered the chance to work for them full-time. I agreed to a meeting and a time was arranged for me to go and see the managing director for an interview. The interview went well and I was formally asked to join the company as their maintenance engineer. The package they offered was fair and I agreed and accepted their offer. Now I was a paid employee again, working for the company that I had been contracted to. Life was even better now: regular salary, all the perks that come with working for a good company such as paid holiday, company car, health cover and pension. I decided I had made the right move.

The next eighteen years were fairly smooth running. Life in general was good. We had a lovely home and good holidays. My daughter was still in private education and life was great. My wife quite often said to me, "I love my home. Where else could I wake up to such a gorgeous view over the river."

Don't get me wrong, on the whole life was good, but there were drawbacks from time to time. One particular problem could have been disastrous for us all.

6

The Wrong Approach

Bitterness is a cancer
Love yourself to love others
Forgive yourself to forgive others

My sister Rosa was a lovely young girl, but as she grew up she developed irrational tendencies towards certain aspects of her life. She would fold all her pound notes up the same way and stand them in her purse just like a row of soldiers. Her tea towels would all be folded the same way and if they did not look correct she would fold them again.

This was all part of her quirky nature, which made her different. It made her an individual.

Sadly, Rosa did not have a happy life in all respects. Her first marriage ended in divorce. Her second marriage was a rebound from her divorce but she tried to make a go of it just as she had done with the first. Unfortunately, Rosa was a magnet for the not-so-nice man and she sadly attracted two, one after the other.

Eventually things came to a head within her second marriage and a divorce was applied for, but Rosa was taken ill and diagnosed with a brain tumour before the divorce was finalised. Through the power of prayer by my mother and others, Rosa lived another three years even though on the night she was rushed into hospital the consultants were adamant that she would not live another twenty-four hours.

The following three years were very difficult for me to cope with. The two of us had been close while we were growing up, doing lots of things together. Rosa use to make mud pies when we were little and make me eat them! If I didn't, she would twist my ear until I obeyed. Some would say that this was abuse, but it was all done in fun and we had a wonderful relationship.

One day Rosa and I went for a walk down some country lanes in our neighbourhood and we came across a box of balloons. We decided the balloons had just been dumped on the side of the road in a hedge, so we took them home as we would be able to have great fun with them. Naturally, we were concerned that Mum would want to know where we had got the balloons from but hoped that she would not mind and allow us to keep them. When we got home Mum was not there, so we decided we would go in the bathroom and blow up some of the balloons. I was only nine years-old and Rosa was ten and a half, but we were intrigued that the balloons were all individually wrapped and they were all the long balloons, no round ones.

We set to work trying to blow up some of the balloons but found them very difficult to blow up indeed, so much so that we did not achieve blowing up any of them! Just before we stopped trying to blow them up Mum came home, found us in the bathroom with all these balloons and said, "What are you doing? Where did you get those from?" Mum calmly but maybe embarrassingly explained to us that they weren't balloons as we had thought, but they were something that a man would use. Maybe that was why the name Durex was written on the side of the packet. The ones that had been opened were thrown away and we were made to take all the others that were still in boxes back to where we found them and put them back in the hedge.

Oh! What innocent days of childhood. We really thought they were balloons. How lovely it was to grow up in such innocence. The world really has changed.

My inability to cope with Rosa's illness during the last three years of her life had an effect on our relationship. Rosa lived near the paper shop I went to daily to get the paper, and she would have been able to see me through her window, sitting in her specially adapted armchair to which she was virtually confined. I, on the other hand would not have been able to see her, due to the net curtains obscuring my vision. I had built up a wall inside me against her illness, as I wanted to remember her as my sister Rosa, not the person the drugs were turning her into. I could not bare the thought that my big sister could die so young, and I not being right with the Lord, was handling the situation very badly.

The time came when Rosa was moved down to my mother's house so that she could be looked after twenty-four hours a day, if required. One day when I called into Mum's to see Rosa, she was in bed, as she quite often was. I went over to see her and she whispered in my ear the words, "I bloody hate you!" I know she did not mean what she said, as it was the drugs talking. She had reason to say it, as I had neglected her in her time of need. I just could not cope with what was happening to her. I was dealing with her illness very badly and it was having an effect on our relationship. After about eighteen months Rosa went back to her own home. The end was not far away and a decision was made that she wanted to die at home, not in a hospice where she went from time to time. It was still an issue for me to call in and see her; I did from time to time but nowhere near as much as I should have done.

One morning, just a few months later, I received an early morning phone call from my mother to say that I had better go up to Rosa's house, as it did not look as though she would be with us much longer. I jumped out of bed and went up to her house, but she had passed away just before I got there. I had said goodbye the previous evening as we had not expected her to last through the night. This, however, did not prepare me for the loss that I felt that morning. I had managed to hold it all together throughout her illness, but I had clung on to the wrong approach. I had been concerned about me and how I would feel when she was no longer here, instead of being there for her as a brother should. I had promised Rosa that I would look after my niece Pamela and I used this promise to keep me strong. I was also there for her husband who had only held onto that status because the final divorce document had not been signed due to the illness. I was there for Pamela when she needed me, as and when storms blew up between her and her stepfather.

A few weeks after the will had been read and the raging had died down, everything that had been going on inside me over the past three and a half years took its toll. I had a breakdown and was off work for a period of three months. I know that the first couple of weeks were spent sitting in an armchair gazing into space, but after that I have no recollection as to what I did during that time. My mind is a total blank, just as if it had all been erased. I know that the Lord was with me even then because I remember waking up one morning knowing that I was okay. I did not realise that God had healed me; I just felt better and it was instant. I went to the doctors and he agreed to sign me off but he wanted me to take another two weeks just to make sure I was well enough. I told him that I was fine but I agreed to take another week to make sure. The following week passed without any hitches or relapses and I went back to work to get on with my life.

Depression, stress, breakdown – call it what you like, it was on my medical record as stress. I could not care less. I knew that I was fine physically because everything worked except for my mind. This had shut down, which is the body's way of protecting itself when it cannot take anymore. You can only get back to normal when the mind decides that it is time to carry on.

I went back to work but over a period of many months, I knew that something was not right. Inside, I was turning into something that I did not like. There was an aggressive streak that was manifesting itself deep within me and it was scary. As I had done before, I buried it deep so that I did not think about it. I noticed that these aggressive thoughts would surface from time to time when a certain subject was raised in any form. It took three years for me to accept what was causing it and a further four years for it to subside.

Now I know you're itching to know what it was that had caused this manifestation deep within me, so I will tell you. It was bitterness. I had been holding resentment against my sister's husband for all the pain that he had caused Rosa and Pamela.

The aggressive streak was making me feel that I wanted to run him over, if I ever saw him and rip his head off if the chance ever came along. I just wanted nasty things to happen to him and those feelings lasted for another four years. I did not like who I was becoming. I was like two different people – mostly nice as I usually was, but when I thought of him I turned into this monster inside. Fortunately, I never saw him after the reading of the will and he has never crossed my path since, even though he does not live far from my mother. This aggressive streak stayed within me until I came back to the Lord. Even then, I had work to do before healing came my way. Through the teachings I received at church, I realised through one particular session that I could not forgive him until I could forgive myself; because I had contracted a cancer, and that cancer was bitterness. I prayed to the Lord asking him to give me the grace and wisdom to enable me to forgive myself and the Lord released me from the bondage that I had brought upon myself. The bitterness went, the anger subsided, the resentment disappeared and all that was left afterwards was forgiveness for myself and for him.

7

Paralysis

My dependency swept from beneath me,
What new adventure doth life lay before mine eyes

Paralysis – now there's a scary word. I had been working for this company for around fifteen years and had to go to Essex one particular Wednesday morning. When I got up, I felt just a slight twinge in my back but really thought nothing of it. Having got ready, I set off for work as usual. The journey was relatively uneventful. On arrival at my destination, I parked the car and went to get out of the car but realized straight away that something was wrong! Standing up was painful and walking was even more painful, but I made my way up to the house I was doing work on and let myself in. By this time I was in agony and decided that I would not stay but make my way home again. I duly left a note and made my way out to the car and sat down. It was uncomfortable to say the least. How strange I thought, what could possibly have happened between home and my destination to cause me so much pain. As mentioned, I had a twinge of a pain in my back when I first got up, but that is all it was. Nothing had given me any trouble during the journey whatsoever. It did not make sense to me – I was baffled. I decided I could not just sit there in the car so I made a start for home.

The journey was a nightmare, as I felt every little lump, bump, twist and turn. I had no choice but to endure it and could not wait to get home and collapse into bed. Thinking back to the outward journey which was so uneventful, I can see that it was the calm before the storm. When I eventually arrived home safely, I got myself back into bed. I contacted the company and told them what had happened and that I would be taking a few days off to get things sorted out, hoping that within a week I would be back at work. I arranged to go and see an osteopath in the town where I lived. He checked my skeletal frame all over as it was the first session, and then made an appointment for me to go back in a couple of days. The osteopath then told me that I had damaged some vertebrae in my spine but he would be able to correct everything over a period of weeks. Over the course of the first two weeks the pain in my spine got progressively worse, and I instinctively knew that this osteopath was not doing me any good whatsoever, so I stopped going.

I decided that I would go and see the doctor and get him to refer me to a private consultant, as I was covered under my company private health insurance. Thanks to the efficiency of private health care I only had to wait about three days before seeing the consultant, but during the wait my pain worsened to the point of agony. I was walking like an old man with severe osteoporosis. I managed to get myself to the hospital on the day of the appointment with the consultant but I remember wishing that I was lying down. The consultant examined me and said that he wanted another colleague to look at my back. All the time this was going on I had no idea what was wrong with me. The consultant's colleague eventually came in and examined me and the joint decision was that I should be referred to the Blackheath Hospital to see another specialist and to be given an MRI scan on my spine. As I was waiting for the appointment, which was unfortunately another week, things got worse and I did not have to wait to be told what was wrong. To a certain extent I already knew.

One morning, I went to get out of bed and I put one foot on the floor followed by the other, which is normal. Getting my legs off the bed was not a problem, so I was really taken by surprise by what happened next. I stood up and immediately fell over! There I was, sprawled on the floor with a big grin on my face. Now having the sort of sense of humour that I had, I started laughing, thinking I was not really awake and had just got off the bed a little too early. I pulled myself up and sat back on the bed. I tried again and stood up and as soon as I was on my two feet, I fell over again. This time I did not laugh, even though I was beginning to feel like a skittle on a piece of elastic. I got up again onto the bed but this time I got into it and stayed there. My mind was going through all the different scenarios of what could be wrong, but there was no point in trying to second guess anything. I decided to stay in bed for a couple of days and rest before I went to the hospital again, which was three days away. When I eventually got up I did not fall over but I was very unsteady on my feet. The following day, I got ready to go to the hospital and was taken there by my wife, as it was impossible for me to drive myself. We checked in at the out patients and were directed to the area where the scan would be done. I had heard stories of being inside a machine where you went through a long tunnel and the amount of time that different people had been in there for, so I did not really know what to expect.

The scan machine was not scary to look at or lie in. The lady who did the scan told me that not all people felt comfortable in the machine and quite a high percentage apparently found it claustrophobic, as there is not a lot of room inside. I knew I did not suffer from claustrophobia so that would not be a problem. I had been told that depending on the sort of scan I was having, I may have to hold my breath for short periods of time and things like that. I tried to keep an open mind about it and found out that there really was nothing to it. My scan took about twenty-five minutes. I had to lie down on my stomach and try not to make any sudden movements, or if possible not to move at all. I must admit that I wondered if I could lie still that long, but to my complete surprise I fell asleep. I had in fact fallen asleep so deeply that the operator had to wake me up when the scan was finished. "Well, that's a first!" she said.

I had to wait an hour before I saw the specialist. When I went in his room, he asked me to strip down to my underpants and proceeded to measure my legs in different positions, prodding me about and testing various reflex areas. When he finished, he started doing his sums, comparing measurements and looking at charts. He then told me that my left leg was two inches thinner than my right, but he did not know the reason why. He wanted me to see a neurological specialist who dealt in tropical spinal diseases. Firstly though, I had to arrange to go and see a chap who would wire me up and send electrical charges into various areas of my leg. The appointment was for a week later, so I waited patiently for the time to come. My wife came with me again, as I was still not solid on my feet. In fact my left leg was behaving most peculiarly. It did not go forward – it went to the left and then forward, rather like a quarter circle sweeping motion! I eventually managed to get into the car and we went to the hospital, so that I could be wired up to the national grid.

When I was a young lad I remember seeing a few people walking the way that I was walking now. I used to quietly make fun of them because they were different. Now though, I know better and will always have compassion for them.

The specialist chap was a young Irishman, probably in his late twenties. Once again I stripped down to my underpants and sat on the chair that had been provided. He started to stick little needles into my leg at various locations and then one by one a wire was attached to the needles, with an electrical charge passing through them one at a time. He told me the reason for this was to see if the corresponding nerves and muscles were working correctly together. The testing took around an hour to complete and then I was sent to another consulting room to see the neurological specialist. Also another young Irishman, probably in his mid thirties but quietly spoken and very concerned for his patient. He said that from the results that he had, it was not possible for him to make a completely accurate diagnosis so he wanted me to have a lumbar puncture. This is the withdrawal of spinal fluid from the lower back with a hollow needle, to be used for diagnosis. Yet another appointment had to be made; more time to wait to find out what was wrong with my body, which by the way had always been fit and healthy, apart from any damage caused by smoking. I had to wait a couple of weeks for the appointment but when it came through, it was within a few days. Chrissie would have to come with me again, as I would need her support after the lumbar puncture.

I was taken into a private ward and asked to undress and put on a gown that was open at the back. The consultant came in, sat down and started to explain to my wife and I exactly what he was going to do and what may happen afterwards. My wife decided that she could not be present while the procedure was carried out, so she went outside. I was asked to sit on the edge of the bed and draw my knees up, tucking my heels into its edge. I had to place my arms around my knees and keep completely still and quiet. I thought to myself, it's alright for you telling me to keep quiet, you're not the one who will have a scaffold pole shoved in your back. When you consider the instruments that could be used the mind does boggle somewhat.

Contents of a spinal or lumbar puncture tray:
Sterile gloves
Antiseptic solution with skin swabs
Sterile drape
Lidocaine 1% without epinephrine
Syringe, 3 ml
Needles, 20 and 25 gauge (ga)
Spinal needles, 20 and 22 ga
Three-way stopcock… Stopcock! What – is this guy a plumber?
Manometer
Four plastic test tubes, numbered 1-4, with caps
Sterile dressing
Optional: Syringe, 10 ml

Thankfully the consultant gave me a local anesthetic before the procedure and we just waited a few minutes before he was ready to start. Now the anesthetic had obviously dulled any pain, but I could still feel the sensation of touch. My mind had started to wonder what he would be doing with a tap, sorry stopcock, but I decided that I would not dwell on what could be just try and relax, ha, ha, ha.

I could feel his fingers searching for a particular spot and when he found what he wanted, I was quietly told that he was about to insert the needle into my spinal cord. Just at that precise moment, my left foot came out of its position on the side of the bed. Perhaps I had relaxed too much as my body jolted and I heard quiet voices behind me saying, "You must keep perfectly still." I retorted with, "Is it ok for me to breathe?" before reassuming the position and the consultant prepared himself for this delicate manoeuvre. This time, I made sure that I did not move a muscle. I was so intent on staying perfectly motionless that it actually gave me a backache. I spoke a couple of times but was politely told by the nurse to be quiet. When the consultant had finished, I could breathe again. Prior to having the lumbar puncture, quite a few people told me that would be very painful. I can honestly say that there was no pain before, during or after. The worst part for me was not knowing what was going on behind me, even though I had been talked through the procedure. It is a little unnerving to say the least. After the lumbar puncture, I had to lie down in bed for an hour, this is obligatory because of the fluid that is drained out of the spine. One of the side effects can be a very bad headache, but fortunately I didn't get one. The fluid would be sent for testing and they had to wait until the results came back, so the consultant made another appointment for me to return. I had now been off work for over two months and still did not know the cause of my illness, but this was about to be revealed.

The letter arrived a week later on the Monday and an appointment had been made for that Wednesday. I was able to drive myself to the hospital without any trouble, which, as far as I was concerned, was a step forward. I sat myself down in the waiting area and it seemed like ages before the consultant called me in. Eventually he came out and escorted me into his office. I sat down and was offered a cup of coffee. The consultant asked me two questions: firstly, whether I used a mobile phone and if so, for how long? Then he asked me if I had been to the Caribbean or any other tropical countries lately? Well, the answer to both questions was yes. I had been using a mobile phone for nearly fifteen years and had come back from the Dominican Republic about four weeks before the pain in my back started.

He mused for a while, then sat back in his chair and said that my left leg was completely paralysed, either caused by fifteen years use of a mobile phone or my recent holiday to the Dominican Republic. Then he said that I had contracted a spinal virus which attacks the spinal cord and causes nerves to die. In my case, all the nerves in my left leg were killed by the virus and this particular virus was prominent in that part of the Caribbean, but could also have been caused by a reaction in the brain from prolonged usage of a mobile phone. He told me it was not possible to say which one had actually caused the virus but it was definitely one or the other. He concluded by saying that the nerves in my leg would grow back but that they rarely grow back in the right place.

I asked him if he could be more specific and he gave me a verbal picture. He asked me whether I recalled the way my leg moved when I told him that I was walking funny. When I said yes he said that the nerves in my leg had already started to grow back, but the nerve that receives the message from my brain telling the leg to move forward has grown to the wrong area, and it is telling my muscles that my leg wants to go out to the left. "Oh ,brilliant", was my own retort. "I'm going to be walking like a pregnant ostrich."

He quickly assured me that this would not be the case as the nerve had already started to grow in another direction. A slight smile came across his face, at my comment about the pregnant ostrich. He continued where he had been forced to stop after my comment about South African wild life. All the nerves would eventually grow back, he said, but he could guarantee that I would somewhere along the line end up with a limp. He was unable to comment on the severity of the limp, as he did not and could not know which nerve or nerves would end up deviating from their targets or where they would end up. He concluded this unwelcome knowledge with a chirpy, "Of all the people I have seen over the years with this virus, none of them have escaped the dreaded limp."

I liked this guy because we shared a similar sense of humor. The big difference was that when he said I would end up with a limp, I thought to myself, that's what you think mate! This guy is limping nowhere! I had to use a walking stick for a couple of weeks, but today, by God's grace, I am fully recovered from that viral attack. In fact, I was fully recovered within twelve months and there was, is and will be no sign of a limp!

Thirteen years later, I am still totally healed from that partial and short term paralysis and by God's grace I'm fitter today than I was then, albeit older. It's not until we lose something we have that we actually miss it and through this temporary illness I have come to realize how important my body is. No, I have not joined a gym to keep fit, but by God's grace I have given up smoking after forty-eight years, and yes, if you work it out I started to smoke when I was eleven years-old. I have however stopped for nine months and have told myself that I will give it a year and then find the appropriate keep fit regime for me and follow a fixed program to maintain my fitness, which is not bad anyway, but could always be improved.

At the end of the day, we owe it to God to look after our bodies as they do belong to him. We are only using them for our short time on His earth.

8

Life as Normal

Light dawneth on my horizon, but
Pitfalls still plot the way

After fourteen weeks, I was back at work. I had, however, become accustomed to being at home. Prior to my virus taking hold, I had been busy at home in the evenings and at weekends, extending my property to the side and rear. I did not want to get involved in the structural side, so I had builders come in and carry out the work up to the topping out stage, or in other words a finished roof. The rest I was prepared to do myself and being more than capable, I enjoyed doing it even with a wonky leg!

My main work was secondary in my mind at this time. I could not wait to get home from work so I could start on the extension to the bathroom, or the new downstairs toilet and shower room. If it was dry, I could go outside and carry on with the footings for my new conservatory. I was enjoying it all and was spoilt for choice.

My work was getting to be a bore, mainly because my line manager was a male chauvinist in the greatest sense of the word and our personalities clashed. I had never met such a bigoted person in all my life! The company I liked, but sadly they were soon to be taken over by an American company which stripped the assets and got rid of 99% of the employees.

We were all given our redundancy notices and it became a waiting game. The time to D-Day ticked away very slowly for me and I had no heart in my work at all. On the day I was due to depart, my line manager could not even bring himself to be around to wish me the best in whatever I did. I learnt a lot of things from him about what not to do if I am ever in a position of leadership.

Now that I had been made redundant, I had time on my hands. The redundancy pay for eighteen years was fairly derisory but it was better than nothing at all. I decided to take some time off work to get the building work finished. After three months all the work had been finished and we could enjoy the extra facilities which had been added to our home. Top of the list for me was the new whirlpool bath I had installed. It was brilliant but only in small doses.

We were enjoying the conservatory that had been installed the year before but I think my wife was getting itchy feet. She had seen a house for sale at the top of the road where we lived and asked if we could go and have a look. She arranged a viewing and we went along to have a look the following weekend. The property was laid out in a very Mediterranean way inside and out. It had a nice appeal and looked out onto the surrounding countryside. We looked into a few things and realized that one of the reasons the owner was moving was due to the excessive cost of having a cesspit rather than being on main drainage. After careful consideration, we decided that it was not for us. So we let the gentleman know and bowed out. Two more properties came to our attention and we showed great interest in both of them, but one was not big enough for what we wanted, although it had a beautifully large back garden. The other was in need of major money being spent on it, but there was the great potential of knocking it down and putting three four bedroom houses on the land. Sadly there was no way that I would be able to come up with the funding for a venture like that, especially being out of work. We were surely blessed in whatever we did or wherever we went. But wait, was it all about to change?

Gentlemen readers, please be aware that it can be hazardous to your life to allow your wife and daughter to go shopping together. My two went out together and I bet you can't guess what they came home with and what effect it had. My wife and daughter had gone shopping one Saturday for the usual household requirements – dresses, hand bags, new shoes – all the sort of things that you would expect to find in the fridge or the larder.

Prior to this particular Saturday, we had been talking for a couple of weeks about the possibility of moving. We had in fact looked at a couple of properties but decided that we would be silly to move, as our house was in a good position and in very good order. The decision had been made to stay where we were as the mortgage was low compared to the average. Our daughter had moved out about two years earlier and my wife and I had just started to find each other again as a couple. Life could be enjoyed, even though I had just been made redundant after eighteen years of service.

Off they went shopping, and it was not unusual for those two to be gone for four or five hours in fact, if they had come back before that, I would have known that something was wrong. When they eventually got home, my wife as usual was full of smiles.

"Guess what?" she said. "We have a surprise for you – we've bought a house!"

"WHAT?" I said. They had been looking around some new building sites and had found a lovely house down by the river apparently.

Oh no! My heart sank, I had worked with new properties most of my life, and I disliked them totally to the extent that I'd never want to live in one. All square flat boxes, plain walls and boring. "What do you mean you have bought one, you don't just buy a house like that", was my reply.

"We have put down a holding fee," she said. "I told the woman you would be down tomorrow to put down a deposit."

Oh great, I thought, no discussion, just get your wallet out hubby – charming. I kept mulling this over in my mind for the rest of the day and evening and must admit I was not happy about it.

The following morning I woke up with a different attitude. I had decided that as a family we had lived in two older properties. I knew that my wife had always dreamt of a new house, so I thought that I should not be selfish, and at the very least go and have a look.

The new property was a four bedroomed town house in a desirable location by the river Thames. After looking around the property, which was still in the process of being finished, and then having a look around the actual site and talking with the sales team, we made the decision to move. We were going to do it for financial reasons as it was in an excellent location. If we stayed there for five years it would increase substantially in value, as it was right on top of Bluewater, a shopping centre in the South of England, and the new Ebbsfleet International Station that was being built for the Channel Tunnel rail link.

So, the house and location that I truly loved was to be left behind. We signed up to a part exchange deal with the developer and through their second-hand sales team the house went on the market and was eventually sold to the first couple that came through the front door. We bought our new house and moved in about a year later. On the day of the move everyone was excited, including me. Adrenalin was running high and it can do funny things to you if you're not careful. I was still out of work, although it had been my decision to take a year off prior to the move. I had decided that a total change of direction would be good for me, so I shelled out some money and started to train as a driving instructor. I had been training for about seven months and was due to start my new franchise three weeks after moving. The day of the move came and we were due to take possession of the house at midday, but a hitch had occurred on the side of the building society with the money. It was extremely late coming through and the staff at the sales team actually stayed late because of it. The money came through around 4.45pm and then the rush started with the final handover and the task of moving in. One of the sales girls said to me that she had never known anyone to be so calm on the day of the move, never mind the hold up. Once again, I know now that my calmness was due to God's hand on my life, although being a backslidden Christian at the time meant I wasn't aware of His help.

At this point things were actually looking quite good for the future. New house, new job, happy wife – but there was one main ingredient missing, in fact the biggest one of all. I had not consulted the Lord, I had not asked for His guidance. I had chosen to do it my way so I was on my own. If we choose to do things our own way, the Lord will not stop us. God gave us free will, after all. Had I made the biggest mistake of my life? Let's find out.

For the next three weeks, I was busy doing little jobs around the property and chasing the maintenance foreman to get things put right, that from time to time reared their ugly heads. I then received a telephone call to go and pick up my new car from the driving school. Well I thought, here we go, let's really make this work. I got pupils almost straight away and on the third day of my franchise I went out on my first lesson as a trainee instructor. The adrenalin was pumping again. I was scared, nervous and excited but the lesson went well and I was pleased.

Funny, isn't it, how some things can be short lived.

As I drove home from a day's work, my mind was busy thinking about many things; the main thought was that after nine months of teaching people to drive, I realized I did not enjoy it. Don't get me wrong, teaching people to drive was a challenge and I enjoyed it, but I had come to a point in the job that I had not bargained for. Most of my pupils were at a point where most of the lesson was just practice, practice and more practice. They knew all that was needed to pass the test, but practice was the key. Some of my pupils were very nice but I had quite a few that did not talk a lot. Coupled with the boring nature of practice I found that on two occasions my eyelids were getting heavy and I could easily have fallen asleep. There was no way that I was going to do a job where I could put other people's lives in danger. I decided then and there to give up my franchise and turn my hand back to my old job.

As I continued to drive home, I went past my old house. I used to live there, I thought. Then I had another thought – I wish I still lived there. Alas I did not. I drove on to our new house, and from this point on I could never associate the word 'home' with it. To put it bluntly, I disliked our new house immensely.

Have you ever been in the position where you have moved house and the wife has said she doesn't like it, and cried herself to sleep because she has wanted to move again? Well, apart from the crying, this was me – I took the role of the wife. Every day when it was time to leave work, I did not want to go. I was constantly aware of a feeling in the pit of my stomach. I told my wife that I did not like it where we were living, and her response was, "I knew you would spoil it for me!" Looking back, I can see that this was a dark time for me in the wilderness, but things were to get much worse.

My wife and I never argued. We would have the odd cross word once in a while, but not actual arguments. She had done a lot of training over a twelve year period, and as a result her outlook on a variety of things had changed. She was a qualified psychotherapist, and as such she tended to analyse things, sometimes to my annoyance. Over the years, I thought that her training could only be good for our marriage, which I thought was strong anyway. In fact I found it was having the opposite effect, only I had not noticed it.

My wife had been doing a management job in a huge organisation, which to a certain extent my daughter and I had pushed her towards, saying she should apply as it would be good for her career. After working in that capacity for about a year, I started to hear the same moan every week – "I don't think I can do this job anymore," and "you don't understand how stressful it is." I heard it so many times that I started to ignore it.

One day, she came home from work and said to me, "I think I'm having a breakdown." Thinking it was the same complaint but in a different form, I ignored it. Then, from nowhere, she started on at me about our dog. I thought, I can't put up with this, so I went out, as I was afraid I would say something that I would regret.

Driving around trying to calm down, I realized that I was getting angrier and I ended up staying out all night and sleeping in a car park. I got home around half past eight the following morning and the house was empty as Chrissie had gone to work. That evening she told me she could not believe I had stayed out all night after she told me she was having a breakdown. She had decided she needed to go away for a few days to sort out her own mind. When she came back four days later, my life was to change forever.

Chrissie told me that she had done a lot of thinking while she had been away and had made a decision. By now I had calmed down and decided that I had behaved very stupidly and had let my wife down at a time when she obviously needed my support.

"Well," I said, "what decision have you made?" hoping that she may suggest that we move.

"I have decided that the marriage is over," was her message.

Wondering if I may have heard her incorrectly, I said, "So you want to separate for a while to sort things out?"

Her reply was, "No, I have made my decision and there is no going back, it's finished."

Twenty-six and a half years of married life, wiped out just like that. I was devastated! When she had finished saying her piece, the words 'boring', 'old', 'should never have married' and 'bad father' were all swimming around inside my head. How could she feel this way about me after all these years?

A few days later when we were talking she said, "I have no doubt that you love me but you are not in love with me. I want more out of the second half of my life, and you don't feature in it."

Well, you can imagine what that did to me. Devastated was not the word. I was in a new job which I did not like, I had reluctantly agreed to move from a house which a lot of people would have given their back teeth for, I was living in a house that I disliked and my wife did not want me in her life anymore. I said to her, "So you want a divorce then."

"No! I shall never get married again, so why should I want a divorce? No, I want to separate and for you to move out."

Brilliant, I thought, now she even wants to keep me hanging on a piece of string; I was most certainly not going to put up with that. "Well', I might want to get married again in the future."

Then she could not make up her mind about what she wanted to do. I thought to myself, I can't cope with all this, and over the next few days I could feel some sort of depression start to creep in. Great, now I'm losing my marbles, I thought to myself.

All was not lost; life was just about to change yet again.

Dear reader, how many of you can relate to any of what has been mentioned over the last few pages. We are all guilty of not listening to our wife, husband, partner, boyfriend or girlfriend. We hear but we take no notice of what is actually being said. When we are courting we proclaim that we love each other intensely. We continue to say the words to each other in text, phone call, email or snail mail. We get married and proclaim it again in front of witnesses, relatives and friends. However, as the honeymoon period comes to a close, which it will, there is some kind of shutter that starts to creep between us that goes unnoticed. I can say this because as I look back I can see exactly where I have gone wrong through the eyes of our Lord Jesus. He has shown me my failings within marriage and they are many. We fail to listen, we fail to look, we fail to understand, we fail to reciprocate, fail to be in love. This is only a small selection of the failings trap that we can fall into. Where does the honour go, the understanding, the humour, the romance? All the good things that can be associated with a loving marriage come from God. If they are not there then we can safely say we are in a marriage that does not have God at its helm. In two chapter's time you will read that God has given me a second chance. I will put everything I have into the future marriage and it will be built on solid foundations of a spiritual nature. I know in my heart that it will last and I know it will be wonderful. Great things will be afoot and I have no doubt that God is moving in a big way.

I'm getting ahead of myself again.

Poem

Foreseen So Serene

There are no clouds, the sky is bright but not blue.
The atmosphere is so full, full of love,
The fruit hangs from the branches on the trees; they are laden beyond that which I have ever seen before.
Colours never known to man, awe inspiring, everything so clean.
There are no seasons, it is continuous, bright warm and loving.
I lay my head down on the grass, it feels like velvet but is green so serene.
A lion lays his head next to my arm already stroking the lamb, they look at each other and close their eyes, and they are at peace.
My brothers and sisters are everywhere, talking and walking, laughing and playing, smiling, ah yes, so very happy.
There is much space betwixt them but they are not far away.
This space is a void full of love, it hangs in the air; there is far more than enough to share.

*It falls from the eyes this love, it is all inviting,
you are welcome everywhere.
The streams that meander through the
meadows, the beautifully cascading waterfalls
are so graceful that love permeates from the
air that they move as they flow.
As I walk a raven lands on my shoulder and
gently brushes its beak across my chin,
You may ask what place is this person in, this
place as foreseen is Heaven.*

R.O.R

9

The Way Home

To deny in life is to gain in death,
The full truth is within my double edged sword,
Cover to cover.

Was there a silver lining to all this? If there was I could not see any, but God had plans.

I was at home out in the back garden feeling very down indeed. I thought to myself, I can't cope with all these feelings and I cried out to God, "Please help me!" The hand of the Lord actually touched me – I could feel his arms around my shoulders in a loving embrace and I could hear him saying to me, "Robert, it is time to come home."

There was no audible voice, just a recognition in my heart that the words had come from God. I just knew yet again that God was there with me but this time it was different, like I was being pulled back into line by the softly spoken loving voice of a caring father. God knew I was unequally yoked and now He saw His chance and took it.

I decided to give my wife time to sort out her feelings even though mine were smashed to pieces at this point.

Three weeks went by and then I asked her what she had decided. She had still not made a decision, so I decided that I would make a decision for her, and I contacted my solicitor and started divorce proceedings. Nothing was contested and we were divorced within seven months.

During this period, I stayed in the marital home and on one occasion, I got very depressed. I was in the back garden and I cried out to the Lord for help and asked him to lift the darkness that was enveloping me, and within five minutes I was back in the house, singing and dancing around whilst drying up the dishes in the kitchen, as if I did not have a care in the world. I moved out once the divorce had been granted and the Lord has been working in my life ever since. I hold no malice toward my former wife. In fact, after the initial mourning period we started to rebuild a friendship. After all, she is still my daughter's mother and always will be, so there needed to be a bond between us for our daughter's sake.

That was Christmas 2004, and for the first eighteen months, I struggled with the loss of my marriage, which was a bereavement, and also with the fact that the Lord had spoken to me about going to my local fellowship. I was not ready to go back to a church with all those strange people. Eventually, one Sunday evening in June 2005 I found the courage to go there on my own. I only just made it, as I was desperate to walk past the door. My body was guided though, and I turned into the church. Praise the Lord, he started healing me immediately, it was like coming home. Yes, I felt scared, insecure and all the things that anyone would feel on going somewhere new. I have now been back with the Lord for four and a half years and my faith is getting stronger all the time. One thing which never ceases to amaze me – when I fall in my walk with the Lord, he picks me up and stands me on my feet again, but I am always at a higher level than I was before. It's like you have to go through a period of learning before you can fail and be promoted. Totally opposite to the way the world works – as I mentioned in an earlier chapter, God uses the weak to confound the wise.

Having settled in my new church, I got to know a few people and then set about making friends. On the first week I was there a lady came up to me and asked me if I was Mrs Russell's son, Robert. I said I was, and it turned out that this lovely lady used to go to prayer group and other meetings with my mother and that she had actually been praying for me to come back to the Lord for over twenty years! She was so excited that God had directed me to her church. We have become good friends and I also get on very well with all her family.

Okay, I hear what you're saying, why did it take twenty years for her prayer to be answered? The Lord does everything in his own time, and the reason for this is because God's time is always the right time and on time.

Eighteen months later, I was talking to different people about getting into a home group, or connect group as we call them. I was given a list of different group names and chose the one that appealed to me most. This group was called 'The Vine' and it was run by my new friend and her husband. She was absolutely over the moon that I had chosen to go there, and still has a big smile on her face whenever there is an occasion for her to tell someone the story of how I came to the church and the group.

I talk to Jesus almost every day. I say almost, because some days I wake up and forget and I feel bad all day but then I come to my senses because I know that Jesus is waiting to forgive me. God is good.

To re-track for a moment, during the waiting period for the divorce I went into partnership with a friend of mine and our business started to grow, although slowly. My partner was not a Christian but he did get the Word from me, and after two years he actually asked me to pray for him a couple of times, although he said it in a semi joking way. I know that my prayers are slowly being answered, praise God, even though our partnership only lasted two years. All those years ago, when I was laying concrete patios and building structures, I realised that the Lord was teaching me about laying solid foundations. The business did well while we were together, and I learnt not to try and get my partner to change to my way of thinking. Just plant the seed and then say nothing. I'd let the Lord do His work and eventually my partner would make a suggestion to me and I would think, I've heard that before. Praise the Lord. The reason for the partnership split was purely because of the way things were going, as our work had progressed from domestic to industrial and commercial. To be honest the commercial pace was thought too quick for me and we parted amicably. My partner was of course correct and we still remain good friends.

This parting was to lead me into another area of my life: I decided to become self- employed, doing all that I had done before but remaining on the domestic side. I spoke to the Lord prior to setting up on my own and felt sure that it was the right thing to do, as it would enable me to tithe to my church from business and personal finances, which was one of the desires of my heart. Sometimes we can consult the Lord at some or all stages of a particular venture, and be absolutely positive that we have heard what God was telling us. However, we do not always hear everything that he is saying because we have preconceived ideas. Having consulted the Lord and setting myself up as self-employed, I felt confident that all would run smoothly and expand just as I thought God was telling me it would. Business was really good for the first two and a half years but took a really bad backward step toward the latter part of the recession of 2009 and early 2010. But I had been able to tithe and bless others and the feeling of being able to give with a pure and happy heart is nothing short of wonderful.

It was during this time that I felt God wanted me to put my life experiences down on paper. Some of this had already been done a few years earlier when I wrote my own testimony. During the early months of 2010 while I was writing this book I had to relive all of what you have read, but this I can see was also the Lord refining me for the plans He had in mind for me. It is amazing how God turns all bad things around and uses them for good. He is so awesome in His entirety: the Three in One, The Trinity.

In the five years that I have now been back with the Lord, many amazing things have happened. Some bad things have also happened, which the Lord allowed, as it was all part of my learning process to trust Him and Him alone for my needs. Not my wants, for wants come from the flesh, but my needs He will cater for.

The first thing that I learnt during this period was that in all the years that I had proclaimed to love God, my love had been in my head and not in my heart. I have no doubt at all that I was born again at a young age, but the darkness of this world had taken its toll over the years and my spirituality had not been allowed to grow. Just before I had come back to the Lord, I was invited up to London by a friend of my mother's to a men's breakfast. I had never been to one before so did not really know what to expect. I had been to business breakfasts, so was it the same sort of thing, or was it just a load of old men spurting Bible verses and praying the same old prayers over and over again? Surprisingly it was neither. We were all seated in a large hall – all being anyone who was invited and anyone who came in off the street, as everyone was welcome to have some breakfast and hear people speak and have prayer if they wanted it. There was a brief word from my mother's friend while we were all finishing off breakfast and then we were introduced to the main speaker of the morning. This young man was there to tell us all about how he came to know the Lord Jesus and also what he had come through to get to that point.

The experience left its mark. Mum's friend asked the young speaker if he would also pray for me. He started to pray and placed his hands on my head, and before I knew what had happened I was on the floor shaking and writhing about. The movements got fairly violent and then it happened – out of my mouth came the most gruesome voice I had ever heard. There was no coordination or clarity in what was being said so it was not possible to understand, it was obvious however that I had been possessed by a demon and it was being delivered from me. I will never know what sort of demon it was and to be honest I don't think I want to know. All that I needed to know was that God was there for me again and I had been delivered from a dark and evil force that had taken up residence within my body. Now, though, I love the Lord in my heart, and it has made such a difference to me and the way I see things and has allowed me to grow spiritually in many ways. God has blessed me with the gift of revelation and discernment. I receive many visions from Him. Visions to give to others and visions of what will come to pass, especially within our own local community and the church. My walk with the Lord has not always been easy and still is not easy.

The difference now is that I know in my heart that I can do all things through Christ who strengthens me and whenever I fall, which is more or less daily, I only have to pray for forgiveness and it is given, as Jesus died for my sins. I don't profess to be the greatest at praying for I am not, but as my walk with the Lord progresses, I get stronger in all areas. So much so that the courage for me to be so open about my past can only come from God, which brings me to the bondage mentioned earlier. The area of bondage to which I refer is masturbation. After my childhood experiences I found myself masturbating on an all too frequent basis during my late teens. Since this period I had been worrying inwardly that the experience with Mr Nasty could mean that I was going to turn out just like him – a child molester and paedophile. I blamed myself for what had happened and was so ashamed that I cringed at the thought of me being remotely like him.

Many children who are abused grow up convinced that they themselves will be an abuser. The experience with Mr Nasty had actually caused my relationship with men in general great harm. I found that it was very few men that I felt comfortable with but I always felt comfortable in the company of women. I had noticed that my mind had started to think up images of young girls and I had also started looking at young girls in a way that I disliked. I started to masturbate to try and alleviate this desire within my flesh, but the relief from my own anxiety was only temporary so the masturbation gradually increased in volume and intensity. This carried on right into and through my married life and it was during my mid fifties after my divorce that I realised that I was now approaching the same sort of age that Mr Nasty would have been when I became his prey. I was scared and deep inside still ashamed. I was no longer looking at young girls. That had ceased quite a few years previous, but nevertheless I was wary of what might happen. After coming back to the Lord, I realised as I grew more spiritually mature in the first few months that what I was doing was actually bondage. The amount of times that the act of masturbation had to be done had reduced drastically, but I was not free from the bondage. Release was needed but that only could come from the Lord.

I had over the previous two years come into contact with a couple of women whom I actually felt a great deal about; we were not involved in a romantic way, although my thoughts towards them were deeper than their thoughts towards me. This in itself gave rise to more masturbation to relieve my desire for more than friendship. This however made me realise that according to bible principles I had committed adultery by my actions (Matthew 5: 27-29), even though the adultery was just in my head. I was now in another situation which God did not want for me.

Fortunately, I had my friend at church to whom I look on as my spiritual mother. I spent many hours with her discussing my friendship with these two women. She could see the downside of the friendships, as she had noticed that my spirituality had been cooling off. Fortunately, with her words ringing in my ears and the Lord's intervention these two friendships were to fall away and once again my mind was free from worldly lust.

Towards the end of 2008 my bondage had disappeared and was completely taken away from me, and God was about to show me why.

10

Love from God

I see inside the heart of thee,
A love so strong twixt you and me,
I avail myself at your side
For in God's love we will abide.

Towards the end of 2008 I had been praying to God, telling him that I just could not carry on the way I had been. I told him that I was lonely and needed female companionship but did not want to get into any sort of bad situation again. I had spoken to the Lord about wanting a wife two years earlier and had actually put in my order through prayer, stating the type of person she should be – hair colour, size, shape, temperament, humour – which was then left to the Lord to sort out.

Now the reason that the Lord had not done anything in the two years up to this point is because I had been interfering. So how had I been interfering? Well, when you give something to the Lord to sort out for you, it must be total. You give it over to Him 100% and you don't interfere. Interfering is not just continuing to look for a relationship yourself, it is also wondering about it – has the Lord got anyone for me yet? All this is interfering. When you ask God for help you hand it to Him totally and just wait on him. All good things will be given to you, but in God's time and then only if it is part of his plan for your life.

New Years Eve 2008 was to be a complete turning point in my life. I would be touched by God yet again. My connect group was holding a get together with a few nibbles and drinks, then praying in the new year. God was to show me something special on this night, something which I will never forget. During the evening God showed me the rear view of a woman whom I knew would become my wife.

I know that sounds strange, especially to be able to say it twice. What attracted me was the Godliness that seemed to surround her body. I only saw her once that evening but what God showed me made a very big impression. I saw this vision again about three weeks later in church, but this time God afforded me only a partial profile view. I was mesmerised and intrigued and could not wait to see what she really looked like. My chance came one Sunday again about three weeks later. As I came out of worship she was standing talking to one of the ladies who belonged to my home group. I went over to talk to her and when the moment was right said, "Who is this lovely young lady then?"

I was introduced to Suzetta, and her friend Margaret said, "This is Robert." Then Margaret started to say more about me and Suzetta cut in saying, "I know, you have told me already."

The conversation carried on for a while, during which someone, I'm not sure who, mentioned that there was a night out coming up, which might be quite good. I said nothing, the conversation came to a natural end and we said our goodbyes. When I got home, I went on the church website and found out Suzetta's e-mail address. I asked her if she would like to go with me as my partner for the evening. The night out was about three weeks away and Suzetta said that she would think about it and let me know. Time passed and the event was soon upon us. That week at our home group, which she had recently joined, Suzetta said to me that she had thought about the evening out, but after careful consideration she would have to say no. I was dumb founded, how could she possibly turn down an invitation from a nice chap like me!

That night I prayed to God, asking Him what was going on. "I know that you want me and Suzetta to get together so why has she turned me down?" I asked God to show me if Suzetta was the one for me. I then laid down to go to sleep and the Lord gave me a vision. He showed me clouds above my head, which broke up and re-arranged themselves into a word, and that word was 'Yes'. The word entered into me. He then showed me a vision of Suzetta's head asleep on her pillow and the word 'yes' entered into her. I slept peacefully that night like a new born baby.

Each Sunday after that I would make a point of talking to Suzetta after worship and we also started to strike up a friendship via e-mail, talking a few nights a week. This carried on for about six weeks and during this time my feelings for Suzetta increased to the point of falling in love. Out of the blue one weekday Suzetta said that we needed to meet and we agreed to get together after worship on that Sunday at Bluewater. I know now that the purpose of the meeting on Suzetta's part was actually to push me out of her life for good. However, after talking for about an hour, she actually found herself being drawn in by my spirituality. Now eighteen months on we are very much in love and always will be, for it is a love with a difference. It is a love that has been given to us by God, it is a love that will grow and grow, it is a love that cannot be experienced in the world without God. It is something which cannot really be explained, only felt within the endless love and grace of our Lord and Saviour.

After being together for eighteen months, we still find ourselves sitting on the sofa just gazing into each other's eyes. We both know what the other is thinking on many occasions and very often an answer to a question will be given even before the question has been asked. We know that our love is special for there is always a special calmness between us and it's like we have known each other all our lives. We are not exempt from having disagreements – far from it – as that is part of a relationship, but God's grace will always see you through the awkward times.

God has great plans for us, we know this ourselves and it has also been prophesied within our home group. We both know our love will last the onslaughts from the enemy and will stand the test of time, for God never gives second best. I have already had a vision of how life will end for us, and that is we will die in each other's arms, Suzetta first followed by me a few minutes later.

I think this is such a wonderful match that God has made and still find it hard to believe that we found each other. Our years together will be long and beyond the normal time span. It is hard to understand a statement like that but in God we trust. I have known since I was a little boy that I will live to be a very old man. By old, I mean at least one hundred and twenty years-old, minimum. I also know that my wife will be with me, unless of course we are raptured prior to this time, and to that I can only say Praise the Lord!

Suzetta has one daughter whose name is Danielle. She is fourteen years-old, although wiser than her years she is in many respects a typical teenager, playing one off against the other and always pushing the boundaries. She is someone I feel will go far, as the years of wisdom come upon her. Danielle is a lovely girl, bubbly and larger than life. We get on very well and love each other. This obviously has pleased Suzetta as Danielle is the most important person in her life. Danielle gave her life to the Lord way before I came on the scene, but in 2009 she made her own decision to be baptised in water and it was wonderful to be a small part of that with her. There is also a bond that will strengthen over time between my daughter Shelly and Danielle, but for the moment it is the teenage years that take centre stage because at this time nothing else matters.

11

The Right Way

There is but one loving all caring God,
He is THE WAY, THE TRUTH and THE LIFE. Amen

There is only one way to live our lives and that is the right way, the Godly way. What is meant by the Godly way? Well, I hope I have managed to portray this within the book, but will recap briefly. The darkness that surrounds the world today is from the enemy – Satan.

What is the darkness? In brief it is drunkenness, rape, any form of abuse, unruly children, no boundaries, the lack of commitment to marriage and the state of the church. Anything that is giving the enemy the upper hand, or rather seems to be. The enemy however is not just prevalent in our individual lives. His work can be seen within laws that are made, the day to day running of the country, the care for the elderly, the excessive amount of crime that is so common in this country today and around the world, and the gradual coming together of a One World Government or One World Order.

I hear many stories, from third parties or through hearsay, about people searching for something better. I pray that it is for God but all too often it seems to be for any religion other than Christianity.

Many Christians however go to church on a Sunday and then don't give another thought to God until they get within the walls of the church on the following Sunday. This is just playing lip service to God and is not true Christianity. It is known as religion, and even Jesus did not like religion. What has happened to the healthy fear of God, love in general, checking on your elderly neighbours, giving up your seat on the bus to a lady, not just because she is pregnant and offering to carry someone's shopping?

Today it is all self, self, self and no one else matters. How sad that our society has come to this point. There is so much more to life than being, sad, aggressive, arrogant, bombastic, materialistic, and selfish, to name but a few. True love is so energetic within itself, for it generates even more love, so why be sad and miserable when you can be joyful and happy? Why go through life not knowing where you are going, when you could know exactly where you will be for the rest of eternity? There is an answer to all the questions that could possibly be drawn from the words within this book, and that is there is only one way, which is with the Holy Spirit living within you. Jesus died on the cross for us all at Calvery. God gave His son to die for us all – that shows how much of a caring, loving God He is. There is only one true God and that is our Heavenly Father, and the only way to the Father is through His son, our Lord Jesus Christ. So let us all reach out for the best that we could ever have and follow the correct path. Let's all go The Right Way.

12

My View of the Right Way

*Hung on a cross, pierced of hands, side
and feet. Mocked and beaten, then sweating blood
for you.
This is true Love*

Some may read this book and think this is fiction. One person would never go through all this for someone else, but believe me he would.

There are many millions out there in the world that go through far more than I will ever experience. So why do I feel that God wants me to write a book to try and help people, and hopefully plant a spiritual seed so that Jesus is the one they look for?

Surely there are people out there that are far more qualified to write this kind of book than me. Yes there are, but God has a plan and a purpose for all our lives, if we will only let him live within us and show us the way to live our life through him.

I sent an e-mail to the lady in my life the other day and part of that is relevant to what I am writing here, so I will include the section I am referring to.

My closing thought... I know God uses the weak to confound the wise, but what if someone like me, being weak and taken in by fiction in the form of a book, is actually the wise one, and the wise and strong ones believe the worldly truth, which is actually fiction.

This is part of the last section of the e-mail I sent and my words were part of a much bigger picture. The fact remains that it tells us in the bible that God uses the weak to confound the wise and this is so very true. How many of you have read this book and can say that everything you have ever done had a good ending? If you were to search your hearts, I can guarantee the answer would be 'NO' or 'DON'T KNOW'. An acronym for the word Bible has been circulating around the world in the last couple of years and it is as follows:

Believers
Instructions
Before
Leaving
Earth

The Bible does not say that this is what the word actually means. It is something that man has put together, but personally I feel it is a great way to look at it. The bible tells us that God uses all things together for good. So when we mess up big time God will always turn things around and use them for our good. He only ever wants good for his children and would never bring harm to them. If you don't know God and just live your life according to the world, there is no guarantee that all things will work together for good. You might be told everything will work out, but it never does in the long term. What we do or say today can have devastating implications for generations to come. That is why we owe it to those who will be born after we have gone to get things right today.

Okay! I hear you. Your grand parents have had a wonderful life, they were kind to everybody and never had a cross or bad word against anyone. So how can I say that things will never work out in the world on a long term basis? Jesus said: "Nobody comes to the Father but through me." So why take the chance that you might go to heaven when you die – If you don't there is only one other place left, and that's hell. Nobody in their right mind would want to end up spending eternity in hell. So don't leave things to chance because you have been a good person. Confirm it, have it guaranteed and know that you have a place in eternity with the King of Kings.

Look at the people that we as a nation elect to run things on our behalf, then look at the mess that has had to be corrected over the years to get things back on track. This is the same as in life and with our families. Most people have heard someone say, 'I'll haunt you when I die', or 'I'll put a curse on you and your family'. When things like this are said, they come to pass and may never be broken if the name of the Lord is not called upon. The mouth can be a wonderful instrument or it can be a very powerful and dangerous weapon. It took me many years to realise that. I have gone through life and at times have said under my breath, 'I will never do that' or 'this will never happen to me'. Without knowing it, I have at times put curses on myself or spoken things into being, and they have stopped me from getting on in life. Thank the Lord they have now been broken and my life is moving on at a pace that I never thought was possible.

Please be careful what you say and the context that you say it in. Sometimes it is necessary for harsh words to be used, so I am going to use a word that I would not normally use to show you a very powerful example. Let's say a man is with some friends having a good night out, and someone decides to perform a party trick. The man decides that this trick cannot be done and states that it is not possible to make it happen. The trick is performed and is 100% successful. Everyone applauds and the man shouts out, "Well I'll be buggered." That one word could be the worst thing he ever said – it could have the potential to ruin his life and possibly that of his family and children. He could well have spoken it into being and it could happen at any time during his life.

I know in my heart that Jesus died for me on the cross at Calvary. His blood was shed for me so that my sins could be washed away and that I might have everlasting life. I know that I have all that because I love Jesus and he lives within my heart.

The world we live in today has become very troubled. It needs the best medicine that could possibly ever be administered and that is the love and forgiveness of our heavenly Father. Look at all the suffering that goes on in the world, all the hurt and heartache, unnecessary deaths, the abuse to innocent children and adults, abuse carried out by those in high authority. None of this is necessary – it can all be eradicated, but the world needs to act.

That is why God is using people that the world would never think of using to bring about healing. I was at the point of writing this particular chapter when I finished a book that I had been reading. It is a book of fiction but it is a very powerful book called *The Shack*. This book has had an effect on me personally and I am grateful to the author, Wm Paul Young, for his wonderful work. It was one of the few books that I did not hold on to, in fact I gave it to a young lady in another country, as she had shown an interest in it. She told me her mother was reading The Shack in their mother tongue, but she wanted to read it in English to help her improve her English. That in itself will be a blessing that will come from the book for her. It is the spoken word in print but it has been used in a good way, so I would say that God has blessed this book as it has the anointing of God upon it, and He is using it for His glory. By that I mean people are learning about the Lord Jesus, God and the Holy Spirit because they have been written into a fictional book but in a loving way, and it is an appealing fictional book that has effect on people's lives.

Admittedly not everyone will read it, but out of those that do, many will start to look for Jesus and many will come to know him. In my view, God is on the move and he is using books, the internet and many other ways to get the Word out. Just look at the sightings that are so common today, with people seeing Jesus in wood, brick, stone and bread, to name but a few items. People may not know the Lord but they see a likeness of him in something and His name gets mentioned by someone who may never have mentioned it had it not been for the sighting. This sighting and the mention of His name can trigger something even if it is twenty or thirty years later.

I was recently flying back from Hungary to the UK and I saw the face of Jesus in a cloud. My own mother has recently had new floor covering laid in her bathroom and I have seen the face of Jesus in the pattern. His name is being spoken by many who would have never thought of using it except in a derogatory sense. We are living in powerful times and the world needs to wake up and take note. Those of us who know we are born again may be in a small minority within the world today, even though we are in the millions. If we could count our brothers and sisters that have been taken home to be with the Lord since the beginning of the world, then we would be looking in the billions. We want you to join us and be our brothers and sisters, do the best thing that you could ever do for yourself go the Jesus way, go 'The Right Way'.

Blessings, Robert.

Poem

The Holy Winds of Change

The Holy winds of change doth come to me in many forms,
My God, my Father, my true love continually reforming my life,
He setteth me free from bondage in areas unknown to me,
My life turned round completely for better not worse.

The comfort of my heart cometh from his everlasting love,
Betwixt my God and me there is a bond, a bond of great love,
Something awesome is afoot in the heavenlies as read,
My God, my Father, bestowing blessings upon my body.

His love is greater than any known to that which cannot be seen,
I reciprocate but alas my love faileth him in many realms,

His love so great, his son and grace was given for my repentance,
Acceptance is unconditional and times of failure irrespective.

His blessings in abundance in my life showest with no detachment,
My faith so strong in his love my acceptance of such without question,
Love in its greatest form embedded within my heart and soul,
My mind renewed for his plan, the end result, the goal.

Debris within my soul cleared, far more love to give to my Father and others.
Ruts not repaired but removed, taken from within forever gone,
Visions in clear clarity sent to this unclean but redeemed body,
Alas, I come not close to your purity, I try, I try, I try with aching heart.

Thou still pourest out blessings upon this body, blessings of wonderment,
Thou cleanest me in all areas of life given by you, alas worldly thoughts still come,
Thou cleanest again, more blessings come, I grow in strength again,
Strength upon strength you give, alas I still fall short of worthiness,

My God how you must love this sinner, my failings known, also my worth.

Your blessings of bride to be, more love instilled within, passion renewed in quantities never known before,
It dawns now, the blessings given to show great love and glory to thee within a marriage of your making,
I rise to the abandonment of all except your gift of future bride to be.

Peace and closure brought to past events, no longer within my heart,
The treasures you unlock to be used for your glory, thus I will obey,
I will fail in areas of future times, your grace sustaining me everlastingly,
I give constant praise for all that is given, for the love in my heart that has changed my very being.

Your choosing of one for other is amazing and electrifying,
The supernatural love you give, greater than any ever known before or later,
My God, my Father, my truest love,
all around me surrounding me with encouragement,
Encouragement to stay the walk, I shall not fail; you know I shall not fail.

*By my side your gift taken from rib within,
the rib of man,
A lady of great mind, peace, compassion, and
abundance of love,
My beloved heavenly Father you know no
end, you lavish your love endlessly,
I know I am of your elect, thus your elected
choice be of same mind.*
R.O.R.

Examples

... of the power of the spoken word

Always be careful what you say when you're talking to God or his anointed. Not long after my divorce, I developed an abcess under one of my lower front teeth. Fortunately after prodding it and pressing it, it went away. About six months later, I developed another one which received the same treatment and went away. I developed a third abcess approximately another six months later but this one disappeared on its own a few days later. Unfortunately it left me with a slightly loose tooth. This tooth slowly loosened more over the next two years until it got to a point where I knew I would have to visit a dentist. It wasn't loose enough to just pull out myself, not that I'm that brave anyway, but it was loose enough to annoy. I knew that some sort of help would soon be required.

One morning I was in the shower talking to the Lord, which had become a routine thing, and I had begun to fiddle with the tooth using my tongue. Just at this time, I said to the Lord, "wouldn't it be funny, Lord, if my tooth fell out right now." At that precise moment, I coughed and the tooth shot out of my mouth and down the back of my throat. Quickly heaving I retrieved my tooth, which fell into the palm of my right hand.

In 2008, I wrote to our Pastor saying that our services are sometimes wound down when it is evident that the Holy Spirit is still present and that we should be prepared to honour the Lord whether He is there for ten minutes or two hours. That night the Holy Spirit kept me awake, bombarding me with visions and other thoughts that I had to deal with. I had gone to bed at 12am, and at 2am I said to the Lord that I wanted to go to sleep. The Holy Spirit told me, "I am not finished yet," and I was kept awake till 4am, when suddenly a peace came over me and I drifted off to sleep. God, in his infinite wisdom again was showing me what will come to pass. During the early months of 2010 the Holy Spirit has hit our church in a big way, and God was showing me that I will need to practice what I preach because I would be spending a lot more time in his presence, compared to what I had been accustomed to.

This one is a prime example of when the Lord has not forgotten you, although he may not be in your thoughts.

My knowledge of computers is minimal, and what knowledge I have gained has mostly been in the last eighteen months, while I have been writing this book. I therefore believe that God has opened my eyes in this area, as he knew that I would need extra knowledge, to enable me to complete this task. As I came to the end of the main story, my mind started to think about a picture for the cover of the book. I had an idea of what I wanted but as I was no good at drawing, I decided to look online. As I said earlier, my own knowledge of computing had been very limited, although I knew I wanted more variety of pictures than I used to get from Home Publishing 2000. I decided to download Microsoft Word 2010 and have a look on the clip art. Hooray! I found just what I was looking for.

I copied and pasted it onto a page where I had already written the heading in the font that I wanted. I was happy with the finished product, even though it may have to be altered when I eventually get to a publisher.

I saved my work as I always do now, having had a few wake up calls in the past. A couple of days later I went into the file where I kept the book and to my utmost horror, the book was not there! No way, not possible I thought. I came out of the file I was in and started again, as it could be hidden within a file within a file. Again it was not there, and now the panic started to set in. Surely I had not lost thirty-seven thousand words! I spent ages searching through different files, even though I knew it was not there. I had a brain wave and decided to look in Microsoft Word 2010 but it was not there either. I was now asking the Lord to show me where it was and for some reason I was directed back to Microsoft Word 2010. Here I went into a section of the programme that I had not been into and I was systematically going through different areas. I was getting to the point of thinking that this was a waste of time when I opened a file and there it was, bold as brass before my very eyes! THE RIGHT WAY. Thank you Lord Jesus, you were there for me yet again.

The Right Way

A Personal Word for You

Should you have been helped by this book, then all the pain I went through was a price worth paying.

Your own personal journey may be similar or totally different to mine.

If you feel, however that you would like more in your life then ask yourself if Jesus is what you're looking for. If you can honestly say 'yes' to the above then the personal prayer below is your key to a new life and eternal salvation.

Say this prayer with an open heart and God will hear every word.

> *Dear Lord Jesus, I know that I have sinned*
> *but through your eternal love and grace,*
> *you are waiting for my prayer. I ask you*
> *Lord Jesus to come into my heart today*
> *and live within me. Show me Lord, through*
> *the Holy Spirit, how to be a good Christian,*
> *how to live the life that you want for me.*
> *I thank you Lord Jesus for saving my soul,*
> *Amen.*

If you have just prayed the prayer above, welcome to the family of our Lord Jesus Christ! You are now my brother or sister in Christ, as you are with millions of other people around the world. We may never meet while here on earth but when we come together with the Father, we shall know each other.

You are now a new born in Christ Jesus and just like being a new born baby, you need to be breast fed. Don't dive in and try to devour the Bible, start with a scripture a day and reflect on that scripture and gradually build yourself up. Ask God for wisdom in all you do, for it is freely given. Find yourself a Spirit filled church and surround yourself with like minded people of God. Arm yourself with spiritual books, which can be a marvellous tool for strengthening your faith, but mostly, get to know the Bible, as this is your weapon against the enemy. Seek the Lord in all things. I have made the mistake of not doing this on many occasions because the flesh wants to do things all on its own. As human beings we tend to please ourselves rather than God.

You will from time to time have to accept that you need to change your mind set on certain things that you may have believed in for many years. These times may be times that you want to refuse to have anything to do with. Hear me brothers and sisters, this is the enemy trying to stop you doing something that the Lord needs you to do before he can heal you, and the enemy does not want you to have the healing. If you are having a fight like this within yourself, ask yourself whether what you feel you have been asked to do would harm you in any way. If the answer is 'No' then you will know that this is from God.

Anything that could bring harm to you in the short

or long term is from the enemy and therefore you should reject the thought in the name of Jesus. By accepting Jesus as your Lord and saviour and the Holy Spirit now living within you, you have the God given right to use the name of Jesus, and there is nothing more powerful than this.

You have accepted our Lord Jesus Christ into your life and in Philippians 4:13 The New Rainbow Study Bible, New International Version there is a message for you from the Lord Jesus. It says, 'I can do all things through Christ who strengthens me.'

May the Lord God be with you in all that you strive to achieve in Jesus's name,

Amen.

God bless you.

Robert

The Right Way

Afterthoughts

Having now scanned through the book after finishing, I am sure that there are many readers who will think to themselves that this chap is either accident or injury prone. Well, I would not actually agree with that. However, if statistics showed that I was accident prone then I would be grateful that I was.

The reason for this is simple. I have in the last four years learnt to listen to the still, small voice of God within me, and believe me it is there and does speak to you.

I have now experienced it many times, and have on occasions missed it and still do, however, now that I know what I am listening for I try a lot harder.

When you start to mature in your faith, begin to understand some of the things the Bible teaches and put them into practice, the results that you can experience because of your faithfulness are nothing short of miraculous. But miracles they are not, they are just God blessing his children because He loves them.

Now, though I can't wait to witness a miracle... WOW.

Find out more about the author and his work at
www.belief-books.com